ON THE EDGE
THEY WALK AMONG US

Henry Billings
Melissa Billings

Wright Group

Series Editor: Amy Collins
Executive Editor: Linda Kwil
Production Manager: Genevieve Kelley
Marketing Manager: Sean Klunder
Cover Design: Michael E. Kelly

 **Wright Group**

Send all inquiries to:
Wright Group/McGraw-Hill
130 East Randolph Street, Suite 400
Chicago, Illinois 60601

ISBN: 0-07-285195-3

Printed in the United States of America.

4 5 6 7 8 9 10 QPD 08 07 06

SAMPLE LESSON

To the Student

Strange and unexplainable things happen to people every day. Rumors of ghosts, psychic impressions, and monsters have confounded people for hundreds of years. The stories in *On the Edge: They Walk Among Us* go deep into the mysteries of true crime, unsolved mysteries, and adventure. Escaped convicts live on the run for 20 years. An evil countess bathes in blood to preserve her youth. Moles in the FBI spy for the Russians. Ghosts haunt a Civil War battlefield. The ghost stories remain mysteries. Some of the crimes have not been solved. You may be the person to crack the case.

As you read the stories in this book, you will be developing your reading skills. The lessons will help you increase your reading speed while you improve your reading comprehension, critical thinking skills, and vocabulary. Many of the exercises are similar to questions you will see on state and national tests. Learning how to complete them will help you prepare for tests you will take in the future. Some of the exercises encourage you to write sentence or paragraph responses. As you write your opinions, you will learn to support them with specific examples from the stories you read.

You may not believe that ghosts actually haunt royal palaces. You may think Dracula does not exist. You may know a brilliant person who can't tie his or her shoes or boil water. One thing is for certain: you won't be able to take your eyes off each page until you've read the book cover to cover.

How to Use This Book

ABOUT THE BOOK *On the Edge: They Walk Among Us* has ten units, each of which contains two stories and a lesson. The stories are about true crime, unsolved mysteries, and ordinary people who do very bizarre things. Each story is followed by a page of reading comprehension exercises. These exercises will help you to better understand the article. At the end of each unit are exercises that help develop vocabulary and critical thinking skills. These exercises will assist your understanding of the similarities between the two stories and will help relate them to your own experiences.

THE SAMPLE LESSON The first lesson in the book is a sample that demonstrates how the units are organized. The sample lesson will show you how to complete the exercises. The correct answers to the questions are included.

WORKING THROUGH EACH UNIT Begin each unit by looking at the photograph. Before you begin reading, think about your reaction to the photo and predict what you think the article might be about. Then read the article.

Sometimes you or your teacher may want to time how long it takes you to read a story. You can write your time in the circle at the end of each story. Use the Words-per-Minute Table on page 120 to find your reading speed and record it on the Plotting Your Progress graph on page 121. As you read through the book, you will be able to watch your reading speed improve on the graph.

After you read the article and record your speed, begin the exercises. The comprehension section will test your understanding of what you have read. The vocabulary exercises will include words that were used in both stories. The critical thinking exercises will help you build analytical skills. Some of the exercises will ask you to write a paragraph giving your thoughts and opinions about the stories. Answers to all the exercises can be found in the *On the Edge Teacher's Guide.*

SELECTION 1

Hiding in Plain Sight

To keep track of your reading speed, write down your starting time before you begin the selection. At the end of the selection, record how long it took you to read the story. You can find out how many words per minute you are reading by using the table on page 120. Watch your speed improve by using the chart on page 121.

Kyle Bell was supposed to be in prison. He was supposed to spend the rest of his life behind bars. Bell was a vicious criminal. He had a history of attacking children. In 1993, he attacked and killed an 11-year-old girl. When he was convicted of this murder, many people sighed with relief. Now Bell would no longer be a threat. From now on, he would be safely locked away. At least, that was the plan. Unfortunately, it didn't work out that way.

In October 1999, prison officials decided to move Bell to a more secure prison. That meant taking him from Tennessee to Oregon. Prison officials hired a special bus company to move him. When Bell got on the bus, he was wearing leg irons and handcuffs. It looked as if he couldn't possibly escape. But hidden in Bell's shoe was a key that would unlock his chains. No one knows how he managed to get it.

On October 13, the bus pulled into a gas station in Santa Rosa, New Mexico. There Bell made his move. Using the key, he slipped out of his chains. He opened a hatch door in the roof of the bus, then crawled out and ran away without being seen by anyone.

For the next nine hours, guards on the bus noticed nothing. By the time they realized Bell was missing, he was long gone. Police quickly spread the alarm. They told everyone to be on the lookout for a man with long blond hair and a mustache. They also described the four tattoos that Bell had on his arms and chest. One was a black panther. Another was a rose. The other two were a flying horse and the Grim Reaper. As FBI agent Paul McCabe said, these tattoos were "very distinct."

On October 15, someone matching Bell's description was seen in a Wisconsin bar. But after that, Bell seemed to disappear. For the next twelve weeks, police had no solid leads.

Meanwhile, in late October, a drifter wandered into a homeless shelter in Dallas, Texas. This man called himself Chris Larson. He had short blond hair and a clean-shaven face. At the shelter, he met a woman with five children between the ages of two to thirteen. The woman liked Chris Larson. In fact, she soon fell in love with him. That November, she and her children moved into an apartment with him.

Rick and Mattie Wilson ran the apartment complex where Larson settled with his new girlfriend and her children. To the Wilsons, Larson seemed like a nice man. He worked at odd jobs around the city. He did a little plumbing and worked as a parking lot attendant. In his off-hours, he stayed home and didn't cause any trouble. There were never wild parties or ugly fights in his unit. "They were what you would call model tenants, really," Rick Wilson said. In fact, Wilson liked Larson and his girlfriend so much that he gave them some old furniture and lent them a TV. He also gave them $50 in cash. "I felt so sorry for them," he said. "They really needed it."

What Rick Wilson didn't know, of course, was that Chris Larson was really Kyle Bell. Bell had cut his hair and shaved off his mustache. He had gotten a fake driver's license under the name "Larson." His new girlfriend didn't know his real identity. Neither did anyone else.

Bell might have lived the rest of his life as Chris Larson. But in January of 2000, Rick Wilson turned on his TV and sat down to watch *America's Most Wanted*. At one point in the program, there was a 30-second spot about Kyle Bell. The show told of Bell's crimes and of his recent escape. A picture of him flashed across the screen.

"When I saw his face, my chin dropped to the ground," Wilson later said. "I couldn't believe it." With short hair and no mustache, Bell looked quite different than he did in the picture. Still, Wilson had no doubt that his tenant was the escaped killer.

Wilson and his wife were scared and upset. But they knew what they had to do. "We just thought, 'That man needs to be off the streets.'" And so Rick Wilson called the TV hotline and turned Bell in.

The police soon arrived at Bell's apartment. They didn't know if Wilson was right, but they were following every lead they got. When they knocked on the door, Bell's girlfriend answered. Then Bell himself came to the door. At first he maintained that he was Chris Larson. He showed them his driver's license with that name on it. But the police could tell the license was phony. So they asked Bell to take off his shirt. As soon as he did, they knew he was their man. There, on his arms and chest, were tattoos of a black panther, a rose, a flying horse, and the Grim Reaper.

And so Kyle Bell was finally returned to prison. Luckily, he had been caught before he hurt any more children. As police officer Jim Hughes said, "I think [we caught him] by just following good procedure, because of the good foundation we laid, and dumb luck." He added, "It never hurts to be a little lucky."

When you finish reading, subtract your start time from your end time. This is how long it took you to read the selection. Enter your reading time below.

If you have been timed while reading this article, enter your reading time below. Then turn to the Words-per-Minute Table on page 120 and look up your reading speed (words per minute). Enter your reading speed on the graph on page 121.

Reading Time: Selection 1

_____ : _____
MINUTES   SECONDS

Work through the exercises on this page.
If necessary, refer back to the story.

UNDERSTANDING IDEAS Circle the letter of the best answer.

1. **Why was Kyle Bell being moved to an Oregon jail?**

   A   The Tennessee jail was overcrowded.

   B   *He had to be in a more secure prison.*

   C   His family wanted him to be in a nearby jail.

   D   He was able to escape from the Tennessee jail.

2. **Kyle Bell was able to get far away from the police when he escaped because**

   F   the bus had stopped at a gas station

   G   he had used a key to unlock his chains

   H   no one saw him exit the bus through the roof

   J   *no one discovered he was missing for nine hours*

3. **Based on comments made by Rick Wilson, the reader can conclude that**

   A   Chris Larson was violent to children

   B   Chris Larson often acted suspiciously

   C   *Chris Larson and his girlfriend were poor*

   D   Chris Larson had a phony driver's license

4. **The police found Bell because**

   F   *Rick Wilson called a TV hotline*

   G   he committed another violent crime

   H   he had his tattoos removed

   J   he rented an apartment and started working

SUMMARIZE For each blank, choose the word that best completes the meaning of the paragraph.

moved	escaped	children
recognized	crime	changed

Kyle Bell _____*escaped*_____ from police

in October 1999. He had a history of violent

_____*crime*_____ against children. After his

escape, Bell _____*changed*_____ his name and

altered his appearance. He _____*moved*_____

in with a woman who had five _____*children*_____.

Rick Wilson, the person from whom they rented an

apartment, _____*recognized*_____ Bell's picture on a

TV program.

IF YOU WERE THERE Imagine that you are Rick Wilson or his wife Mattie. Write a paragraph explaining what you would do if you suspected that one of your tenants was wanted by the police. Be sure to include examples from the story to support your response.

   Like Rick Wilson, I would be very frightened.

I would call the police as soon as possible. I would

not confront the person myself. I would wait for the

police to arrive.

Read the next article and complete the exercises that follow.

3

"**A**rmed and dangerous." That's how police described the Texas Seven. These seven men escaped from a South Texas prison on December 13, 2000. The group's leader, George Rivas, planned every move. He and his gang cornered guards one by one. They beat them and tied them up. Then they stole their clothes, wallets, and weapons. Finally, the convicts sneaked out in a truck owned by the prison.

By the time prison officials discovered the break-out, it was too late. The Texas Seven had vanished. The prison truck was later found in a Wal-Mart parking lot. But there was no sign of the men themselves.

The police were worried. All of the escaped convicts were violent. They had been sent to prison for robbing, killing, and kidnapping. One had beaten a baby almost to death. Now they were on the loose. They had sixteen guns and hundreds of bullets. And it looked as if they planned to commit more crimes. They left behind a note for officials to find. It said, "You haven't heard the last of us."

By nightfall, police from around the state were on the case. "Every lawman in the state of Texas is looking for these guys," said prison spokesman Larry Todd. "They may have split up, they may have gone in pairs. We don't know."

For the next day and a half, the police searched in vain. Then, on December 15, George Rivas and one of his partners entered a Radio Shack store in Portland, Texas. They robbed the store of all its money. They also took equipment that would enable them to listen to police radios. Workers at the store identified the robbers as members of the Texas Seven. Now the police had a lead. But since the convicts could listen to police radios, it would be harder than ever to catch them.

The Radio Shack was not far from Mexico, so police figured that was where the gang would go next. Extra officers rushed to the border. But the convicts didn't go toward Mexico. Instead, they moved north. On December 19, they rolled into the town of Farmers Branch near Dallas. Using a false name, they rented a motel room. The desk clerk only saw four of them. She didn't know that three others would also be sharing the room. It never occurred to her that these men were the "most wanted" men in the country.

On December 24, Rivas and his gang struck again. They walked into a sporting goods store in Irving, Texas. They pulled out their guns and began to rob the place. Before they finished, police officer Aubrey Hawkins drove up. The gang shot and killed Hawkins before he could even get out of his car.

Now the people of Texas were really scared. No one knew where the convicts would go next. And as long as the group was at large, no one felt safe. Anyone could be the next victim. People began looking over their shoulders. They jumped at strange noises. Every stranger looked suspicious. People began to imagine they saw the convicts everywhere. The police were flooded with calls. The police knew that most of the tips would be dead ends. But they couldn't take chances. They had to do everything they could to find the Texas Seven.

"To tell the truth, we don't know where they are," said Larry Todd. "We don't even know what car they're driving. We must follow all leads."

As it turned out, the Texas Seven were no longer in Texas. On New Year's Day they had moved to Colorado Springs, Colorado. By this time, they had used some of the robbery money to buy a motor home. So they moved into an RV park. They told everyone they were missionaries. People believed them. The men seemed so nice and polite. Some of them even started going to local church meetings.

Meanwhile, back in Texas, the search continued. Officials thought the gang was still in the state. So fear ran high. Texas news programs ran pictures of the convicts. So did shows such as *America's Most Wanted*. At one point, the faces of the convicts were even put on pizza boxes. People were asked to keep their eyes open and their doors locked.

At last, on January 21, the police got a break. Wayne Holder, the owner of the RV park, saw pictures of the Texas Seven on TV. He thought they looked familiar. In fact, he thought they looked like the men who were staying in his park. Holder wanted to be sure. He used the Internet to look at their pictures again. After that he had no doubt. He picked up the phone and called the police.

The police rushed to the RV park. The seven convicts were not all in the motor home at the time, so it took awhile to round them up. But over the next two days the police arrested six of them. The seventh man killed himself rather than be taken in.

Finally people could relax. For nearly six weeks, the convicts had terrorized the state of Texas and beyond. Now, at last, these men were off the streets. The Texas Seven would never again walk among us.

If you have been timed while reading this article, enter your reading time below. Then turn to the Words-per-Minute Table on page 120 and look up your reading speed (words per minute). Enter your reading speed on the graph on page 121.

Reading Time: Selection 2

_____ : _____
MINUTES   SECONDS

UNDERSTANDING IDEAS Circle the letter of the best answer.

1. Which statement belongs in the empty box?

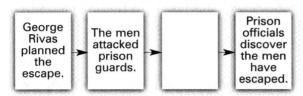

| George Rivas planned the escape. | → | The men attacked prison guards. | → | | → | Prison officials discover the men have escaped. |

A The prisoners escaped in a truck owned by the prison.

B The police truck was found in a Wal-Mart parking lot.

C The convicts' pictures were on pizza boxes.

D Every lawman in the state of Texas was looking for the men.

2. Which of the following words best describes what many people in Texas felt after the escape of the Texas Seven?

F anger

G confusion

H determination

J fear

3. The note that the convicts left behind seemed to indicate that they

A were headed to Mexico

B were going into hiding

C intended to commit more crimes

D would be able to monitor police activity

SUMMARIZE For each blank, choose the word that best completes the meaning of the paragraph.

missionaries	prison	kidnapping
owner	hardened	traveled

George Rivas and six other men escaped from a Texas

_____ in December of 2000. They

were _____ criminals who were in

prison for robbery, murder, and _____.

The Texas Seven, as they were called,

_____ to Colorado, where they

bought a motor home. They were pretending to

be _____. Eventually, the

_____ of the RV park recognized the

men from a TV show and called police.

IF YOU WERE THERE Imagine that you are a member of the police force trying to capture the Texas Seven. Write a brief paragraph explaining how you would try to find them. Be sure to include examples from the passage to support your response.

_____

_____

_____

_____

_____

_____

_____

USE CONTEXT CLUES When you read, you may find a word whose meaning is unfamiliar to you. When that happens, you can look up the word's meaning in the dictionary. You can also find out what the word means by looking for context clues. These are words or sentences that come before or after the word. Context clues can be words with the same or opposite meanings as the unfamiliar word. They may also be an example or definition of the unfamiliar word.

Read each excerpt from the stories you just read. Circle the letter with the best meaning of the underlined word.

1. **They also described the four tattoos that Bell had on his arms and chest. . . . As FBI agent Paul McCabe said, these tattoos were "very distinct."**

   A common, everyday

   B carelessly done

   C clear, unmistakable

   D mean, evil

2. **"I think [we caught him] by just following good procedure, because of the good foundation we laid, and dumb luck."**

   F process, a way of doing something

   G basis

   H fortune, luck

   J tips

3. **For the next day and a half, the police searched in vain. "To tell the truth, we don't know where they are," said Larry Todd.**

   A conceited

   B selfish

   C blood vessel

   D without success

4. **Workers at the store identified the robbers as members of the Texas Seven. Now the police had a lead.**

   F recognized

   G reasoned

   H feared

   J used

5. **Finally the people could relax. For nearly six weeks, the convicts had terrorized the state of Texas and beyond.**

   A arranged

   B controlled

   C frightened

   D traveled

PUT WORDS INTO CONTEXT Complete the paragraph using the underlined words from the exercise on this page.

Everyone in Texas knew that with the convicts on the loose, it was a _____ possibility that they would hurt someone. Only two days after their escape, they were _____ as the men who robbed a Radio Shack. The police made several _____ attempts to catch the men before they were finally successful.

ANTONYMS An antonym is a word that has the opposite meaning of another word. For example, *dangerous* is an antonym for the word *safe*. Circle the letter or phrase that means the OPPOSITE of the underlined word.

1. **Bell was a <u>vicious</u> criminal.**

   A funny

   B bad-tempered

   C kind, good

   D interesting

2. **Rick and Mattie Wilson ran the apartment complex where Larson settled with his <u>new</u> girlfriend and her children.**

   F old

   G recent

   H modern

   J young

3. **But the police could tell the license was <u>phony</u>.**

   A homemade

   B fake

   C genuine

   D expired

4. **But since the convicts could listen to police radios, it would be <u>harder</u> than ever to catch them.**

   F easier

   G stronger

   H farther

   J longer

5. **People began looking over their shoulders. They jumped at <u>strange</u> noises.**

   A creepy

   B familiar

   C odd

   D loud

6. **For nearly six weeks, the convicts had <u>terrorized</u> the state of Texas and beyond.**

   F comforted

   G frightened

   H threatened

   J robbed

ANTONYM ANALOGIES Analogies show similar patterns between words. Antonym analogies show patterns between words that have opposite meanings. For example, *large* is to *small* as *tall* is to *short*. For each blank, choose an underlined word from the exercise on this page to correctly complete the analogy.

1. *Usual* is to *extraordinary* as *commonplace* is to

   _____ .

2. *Ancient* is to *modern* as *old* is to

   _____ .

3. *Good* is to *evil* as *kind* is to

   _____ .

4. *Simple* is to *complex* as *easier* is to

   _____ .

5. *Genuine* is to *fake* as *real* is to

   _____ .

ORGANIZE THE FACTS The two stories you read in this unit are alike in some ways and different in other ways. A Venn diagram can show how they are alike and different. Look at the Venn diagram below. Then choose the best answer to each question.

"HIDING IN PLAIN SIGHT"
Used a key to escape

BOTH
Featured on *America's Most Wanted*

"TEXAS SEVEN"
Beat guards when they escaped from prison

1. **Which of the following details belongs in the oval marked "BOTH"?**

   A recaptured by police

   B shaved his mustache

   C pretended to be missionaries

   D moved to an RV park

2. **Which detail does NOT belong in the oval marked "Hiding in Plain Sight"?**

   F Bell was convicted of murder.

   G Bell eluded police for a little more than a year.

   H Bell moved in with his girlfriend.

   J Bell escaped with six other convicts.

3. **Which detail does NOT belong in the oval marked "The Texas Seven"?**

   A They robbed a Radio Shack.

   B They shot and killed Aubrey Hawkins.

   C They were called "model tenants" by their landlord.

   D Their faces were pictured on pizza boxes.

4. **Which detail belongs ONLY in the oval marked "Hiding in Plain Sight"?**

   F The escape vehicle was a stolen prison truck.

   G Unusual tatoos were used to identify the fugitive.

   H A note was left behind for law enforcement officials to find.

   J A landlord watched *America's Most Wanted*.

CONTINUE THE COMPARISON Fill in the chart with three additional details about how the stories are alike.

More ways the stories are alike:

CONTINUE THE CONTRAST Fill in the chart with three additional details about how the stories are different.

More ways the stories are different:

DRAW CONCLUSIONS A conclusion is a judgment based on information. The way you draw a conclusion is to think about what you already know about the subject and what you've read. Then see if you can make a judgment, or general statement, about it. Read this paragraph about *America's Most Wanted*. Then choose the best answer to each question.

[1] The TV show *America's Most Wanted* made its debut in February 1988. [2] Within four days, the first criminal was arrested because of a tip from a viewer. [3] Two years later, the first missing child was recovered. [4] Since the show first aired in 1988, 714 criminals have been captured as a result of information broadcast on *America's Most Wanted*. [5] The host of the show is John Walsh, whose son was kidnapped and later found murdered. [6] The kidnapper was never brought to justice.

1. **Which sentence from the paragraph explains how successful the TV show has been since it started?**

   A Sentence 1

   B Sentence 2

   C Sentence 3

   D Sentence 4

2. **Which sentences from the paragraph help you conclude that John Walsh is highly motivated to find America's most wanted criminals?**

   F Sentences 1 and 2

   G Sentences 3 and 4

   H Sentences 5 and 6

   J All the sentences

JUDGE THE EVIDENCE When you make a conclusion, you must judge if the information presented is accurate or convincing. Choose the best answer.

1. **Which statement best supports the conclusion that ordinary citizens can help the police?**

   A Sometimes convicts escape from prison.

   B You never know the complete background of your neighbors.

   C Rick Wilson and Wayne Holder both reported escaped prisoners to police.

   D Kyle Bell changed his name to Chris Larson.

2. **Which statement best supports the conclusion that police try just about everything to catch criminals?**

   F Police usually ignore leads from anonymous callers.

   G The pictures of the Texas Seven were on pizza boxes.

   H Police ask questions and conduct extensive investigations at crime scenes.

   J The show *America's Most Wanted* has helped capture hundreds of criminals.

YOUR OWN CONCLUSION What would you do if you suspected that one of your neighbors was in trouble with the law? Support your conclusion with examples from both stories.

_____

_____

_____

_____

_____

_____

SELECTION 1

Off the Charts

ichael's parents couldn't believe it. Their four-month-old baby was talking! Most children say their first word around the age of 12 months. But Michael began speaking at four months. By six months, he was using complete sentences. When his mother took him to the doctor one day, Michael told the doctor, "I have a left ear infection."

Michael Kearney was born in January of 1984. His parents weren't expecting him to be a quick learner. In fact, they worried that he might be mentally retarded. He was born prematurely, weighing just 4 pounds, 2 ounces. The doctor told them that he would likely have developmental problems.

Kevin and Cassidy Kearney hoped the doctor was wrong. In any case, they wanted to help their son take full advantage of whatever abilities he had. So they worked hard to stimulate his mind. They took him with them wherever they went. They talked to him all the time. It turned out that they didn't need to worry. Michael was not mentally retarded. In fact, he was brilliant.

Every day he showed more amazing abilities. By the time he was ten months old, he could read road signs and food labels. In their book *Accidental Genius*, Kevin Kearney describes what happened when he and his wife tried to spell out messages to each other.

"I would say to Cassidy, 'Why don't we go out and get some F-R-E-N-C-H F-R-I-E-S?'"

"Michael would chime in from his baby walker, 'That sounds good. Let's go to M-C-D-O-N-A-L-D-S.'"

When Michael was two, he could read anything that was put in front of him. At age three, he figured out algebra. He had what his parents called a "rage to learn." If they didn't feed him new information, he became restless and unhappy. He wanted to play word games, number games, or spelling games all the time. His father began to spend hours planning new material for Michael to learn the next day. But Michael would master it all in half an hour. Then he would ask for more.

The Kearneys put Michael in kindergarten when he was three years old. They thought he would have fun. They also thought that being with other children might slow down his learning a bit. This seemed like a good idea. The Kearneys wanted their son to grow up to be happy and healthy. They thought his life might be easier if he was more like other children.

But the Kearneys couldn't change who or what Michael was. Each day after kindergarten Michael would beg his mother for new lessons. "Where's my work? Where's my work?" he'd cry. Soon Kevin and Cassidy had to face the truth. Their son was what they called "severely gifted." They had his IQ tested. But the test didn't go high enough for him. He was literally off the chart.

The Kearneys finally decided to let Michael be Michael. They pledged to do everything they could to help his talents unfold. And so they schooled him at home. He raced through the material at each grade level. By the time he was four, he was doing fifth-grade work. At five years old, he was ready for high school material. His parents worried about gaps in his knowledge base. So they gave him tests from Johns Hopkins University. These multiple choice exams were designed to show what a child did or did not know in certain subjects. But Michael was too smart for the tests. Somehow he could figure out the right answer just from the way the questions were laid out. So he got perfect scores even in subjects he had never studied.

When Michael was six and a half, he entered college. By the time he was ten, he was through college and headed toward graduate school. By age 14, he held a master's degree in biochemistry.

Michael wasn't finished, of course. He began working on a second master's degree. This time the field was computer science. He hoped to have his Ph.D. by the time he was twenty.

Meanwhile, Michael's little sister Maeghan was also setting records. She was born just eighteen months after Michael, and showed just as much promise. She, too, had a "rage to learn." An illness in infancy slowed her down a bit. But by the time she was four years old, she was doing third-grade work. The Kearneys home-schooled her just as they had Michael. At age 16, Maeghan was getting ready to graduate from college.

In *Accidental Genius*, Cassidy Kearney wrote, "Whatever the future holds for both Michael and Maeghan is not for Kevin and me to decide. All we want is for both of them to be happy, well-adjusted adults." She and her husband would do all they could to support these amazing children, she said. And she added, "After that, it's up to them."

If you have been timed while reading this article, enter your reading time below. Then turn to the Words-per-Minute Table on page 120 and look up your reading speed (words per minute). Enter your reading speed on the graph on page 121.

Reading Time: Selection 1

_____ : _____
MINUTES   SECONDS

UNDERSTANDING IDEAS Circle the letter of the best answer.

1. Why did Michael Kearney's parents fear that he might be mentally retarded?

A Michael didn't act like a baby.

B Michael was born prematurely.

C Michael had an ear infection when he was little.

D Michael started talking when he was 4 months old.

2. Which statement explains the meaning of Michael Kearney's "rage to learn"?

F He was angry all the time.

G He was an unhappy genius.

H He was upset if his parents tried to teach him anything.

J He was unhappy if he wasn't learning something new all the time.

3. What was one of the biggest problems Michael's parents faced?

A Michael's health as a baby

B Michael's ability to speak at such an early age

C keeping Michael busy with enough new things to learn

D preventing Michael's IQ from getting off the charts

4. Which of the following best describes what the Kearneys want for their children?

F to be happy

G to be well educated

H to get perfect scores on all their tests

J to be the smartest people in the world

SUMMARIZE For each blank, choose the word that best completes the meaning of the paragraph.

information	college	graduated
speaking	amazing	records

From the very beginning, Michael Kearney was an _____ child. He was _____ by the time he was four months old. His parents did everything they could to provide him with enough new _____ to learn. Michael was finished with _____ by the age of ten. Michael's little sister Maeghan has set _____ of her own. She _____ from college at the age of 16.

IF YOU WERE THERE Imagine that you are Michael Kearney's parent. What would you want him to do? Write a brief paragraph explaining your actions. Be sure to include examples from the story to support your response.

_____

_____

_____

_____

_____

_____

Faking It

It seemed impossible. Nobody could be that smart. But Elizabeth Chapman had the test results to prove it. Her son Justin was a genius. He started to walk when he was just seven months old. He learned to play the violin at age two. He could read before he was two and a half. And by age three, he was a great chess player.

Elizabeth knew she would have to work hard to keep up with her son. She was just twenty years old when he was born on July 17, 1993. She had no college degree. She was a single mother with no real career. Yet she vowed not to hold Justin back in any way. She wanted him to have every chance at success.

When Justin was three, Elizabeth took him for an intelligence test. He got the highest possible score. The next year, she put him in a program for gifted students. It was based in California. The Chapmans lived in upstate New York. But that didn't matter. The classes were set up for long-distance learning. Justin simply sent his work in over the Internet.

When Justin was five and a half, Elizabeth found a high school for him. It was in Florida. But it, too, offered long-distance learning. So Justin could do all his work at home. The next step, of course, was college. At age six, Justin started taking classes at the University of Rochester while he was finishing high

school. He was the youngest student who had ever studied at Rochester.

Next, Elizabeth got in touch with Linda Silverman. Silverman ran a center for gifted children in Colorado. She gave Justin another intelligence test. When she finished, she declared him to be "the greatest genius to ever grace the earth." In her own words, she was "blown away." The average score on the test was 100. Anything over 140 was considered gifted. Justin scored 298.

Elizabeth was delighted. She was also pleased with Justin's SAT scores. The SATs are tests taken in high school. Justin got a very strong score of 650 on the verbal section of the test. On the math section, he scored a perfect 800. He was only six years old.

By this time, Justin was becoming famous. He met with the governor of New York. He gave speeches. He also began to write his own newspaper column. He called it "The Justin Report." Everyone was dazzled by this little boy. He truly seemed to be headed for greatness.

But then the problems began. Justin had no trouble reading his speeches. But he could not always answer questions from the audience. When someone asked him to name his favorite color, he couldn't. His mother said it was because he thought of too many possible choices. Others blamed a learning disability. Justin seemed to have trouble processing sounds. That explained why he could read and write but couldn't always carry on a conversation.

In August 2001, Justin and his mother moved to Colorado. There, Justin went to a special school. It was for gifted children who had a disability. But this didn't seem to help. In fact, Justin's troubles got worse. He began to sleep more and write less. He started sucking his fingers. He played with toddler toys. He even threw tantrums in the classroom. Justin told a worker at the school that he didn't want to live anymore.

Soon after that, he was taken to the hospital. Doctors feared he might try to kill himself. They wondered if Elizabeth had pushed him too hard. They also wanted to see for themselves how smart he was. So they gave him yet another intelligence test. The results stunned everyone. Justin scored only in the average range. Hospital workers noted that he could not spell simple words such as "fire" or "get." He could not define the word "sum."

In the face of all this, Elizabeth admitted the truth. She had faked all of Justin's early tests. He hadn't finished the first test. He had done only two out of the thirteen sections. Elizabeth had filled out the rest herself. When it came time for the second test, she again "helped" her son. This time she gave him the answer book ahead of time. He studied it for days before he took the test. As for the SATs, well, he had never taken those at all. She had put his name on a neighbor's test results.

"I just got caught up in it," Elizabeth said. "I wanted to be a good mom and give him opportunities I didn't have. I don't do anything halfway. It was wrong. I made some poor choices."

Charlene Kociuba was Elizabeth's neighbor. She said that Elizabeth put terrible pressure on Justin. She was not the only one who condemned Elizabeth. Many others did, too. They also wondered how she had gotten away with it. It turned out that none of Justin's early teachers really knew him. Most of their contact came through e-mail. The teachers assumed that Justin was doing his own work. But they had no way of checking. The same was true for his teachers at college. The professors gave take-home tests. They trusted that students were doing their own work.

Elizabeth said that Justin had in fact done the school work himself. "He is still a really gifted boy," she said. She also said, "I didn't mean to hurt anyone in doing this." But she had hurt someone. That person, of course, was Justin. It was no longer clear how bright he was. But it was clear that he was miserable. As he told one doctor, "I just don't want to be me anymore."

If you have been timed while reading this article, enter your reading time below. Then turn to the Words-per-Minute Table on page 120 and look up your reading speed (words per minute). Enter your reading speed on the graph on page 121.

Reading Time: Selection 2

_____ : _____
MINUTES   SECONDS

UNDERSTANDING IDEAS Circle the letter of the best answer.

1. Which statement belongs in the empty box?

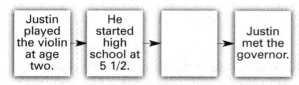

| Justin played the violin at age two. | → | He started high school at 5 1/2. | → | | → | Justin met the governor. |

A Justin threw tantrums in school.

B Justin and his mother moved to Colorado.

C Justin started classes at the University of Rochester.

D Justin started sucking his fingers.

2. Because Justin had trouble processing sounds, he

F was taken to the hospital

G had difficulty reading his speeches

H began to sleep more and write less

J couldn't always carry on a conversation

3. What was unusual about Justin's scores on the intelligence test he took in Colorado?

A He scored in the average range.

B He scored higher than anyone else ever had.

C He was perfect in math, but not as good in English.

D He could not spell simple words such as "fire" or "get."

4. The most likely cause of Justin's misery was

F going to college at age six

G the pressure of being labeled "gifted"

H her mother's admission of faking his tests

J the fact that the doctors labeled him "average"

SUMMARIZE For each blank, choose the word that best completes the meaning of the paragraph.

scores	admitted	opportunities
single	high school	obvious

Justin Chapman was born to a

_____ mother in 1993. It was

_____ that Justin was special.

He was in _____ before he

was six years old. Later, though, Justin's mother

_____ that she had faked some

of Justin's test results. She even said that she had stolen

the _____ for the SAT. Elizabeth

Chapman said that all she wanted was to give Justin

_____ that she didn't have.

IF YOU WERE THERE Imagine that you are the parent of an unusually intelligent child. What would you do to help him or her? Write a brief paragraph explaining your actions. Be sure to include examples from the story to support your response.

_____

_____

_____

_____

_____

_____

USE CONTEXT CLUES When you read, you may find a word whose meaning is unfamiliar to you. When that happens, you can look up the word's meaning in the dictionary. You can also find out what the word means by looking for context clues. These are words or sentences that come before or after the word. Context clues can be words with the same or opposite meanings as the unfamiliar word. They may also be an example or definition of the unfamiliar word.

Read each excerpt from the stories you just read. Circle the letter with the best meaning of the underlined word.

1. **In fact, they worried that he might be mentally retarded. . . . The doctor told them that he would likely have underlined developmental problems.**

   A growth

   B sickness

   C emotional

   D nervous breakdown

2. **They worked hard to underlined stimulate his mind. They took him with them wherever they went. They talked to him all the time.**

   F create

   G deaden

   H excite

   J slow

3. **An illness in underlined infancy slowed her down a bit. But by the time she was four years old, she was doing third-grade work.**

   A pregnancy

   B kindergarten

   C babyhood

   D day care

4. **When she finished, she underlined declared him to be "the greatest genius to ever grace the earth."**

   F asked

   G announced

   H imagined

   J invented

5. **He even threw underlined tantrums in the classroom. He told a worker at the school that he didn't want to live anymore.**

   A threats

   B speeches

   C toddler toys

   D fits of anger

PUT WORDS INTO CONTEXT Complete the paragraph using the underlined words from the exercise on this page.

Once children are _____

geniuses, their lives are never the same. Usually during

_____ parents can tell that their

children are very special. Parents do whatever they

can to _____ the rapid

_____ stages in their children's

minds.

SYNONYMS A synonym is a word that has the same, or nearly the same, meaning as another word. For example, *amazing* and *surprising* are synonyms.

Circle the letter of the word or phrase that has almost the SAME meaning as the underlined word.

1. Michael was born <u>prematurely</u>, weighing just 4 pounds, 2 ounces.
   A sickly
   B past due
   C too early
   D deformed

2. Michael's parents <u>pledged</u> to do everything they could to help his talents unfold.
   F demanded
   G promised
   H refused
   J thought

3. This little boy <u>dazzled</u> everyone.
   A happy
   B irritated
   C impressed
   D upset

4. In the face of all this, Elizabeth <u>admitted</u> the truth.
   F confessed
   G asked for
   H discovered
   J lied about

5. Kociuba was not the only one who <u>condemned</u> Elizabeth.
   A approached
   B believed
   C caught
   D criticized

6. The professors gave take-home tests. They <u>trusted</u> that students were doing their own work.
   F asked
   G believed
   H were doubtful
   J wondered if

SYNONYM ANALOGIES Analogies show relationships between words. Synonym analogies show patterns between words that have similar meanings. For example, *big* is to *large* as *little* is to *small*. For each blank, choose an underlined word from the exercise on this page to correctly complete the analogy.

1. *Exited* is to *departed* as *accepted* is to

   _____ .

2. *Began* is to *started* as *promised* is to

   _____ .

3. *Shut* is to *closed* as *excited* is to

   _____ .

4. *Thrilled* is to *excited* as *blamed* is to

   _____ .

5. *Quickly* is to *rapidly* as *early* is to

   _____ .

ORGANIZE THE FACTS The two stories you read in this unit are alike in some ways and different in other ways. A Venn diagram can show how they are alike and different. Look at the Venn diagram below. Then choose the best answer to each question.

"OFF THE CHARTS"
IQ test did not go high enough for Michael

BOTH
Unusual children

"FAKING IT"
Mother fakes son's early test results

1. **Which detail belongs in the oval marked "BOTH"?**

    A earned a master's degree in biochemistry

    B played musical instruments at an early age

    C intelligence amazed people

    D scored well on the SATs

2. **Which detail does NOT belong in the oval marked "Off the Charts"?**

    F talking at 4 months old

    G has baby sister

    H born prematurely

    J long-distance learning

3. **Which detail does NOT belong in the oval marked "Faking It"?**

    A youngest student at Rochester

    B had a "rage to learn"

    C son of single mother

    D difficulty processing sounds

4. **Where in the diagram does "a child genius" belong?**

    F in the oval marked BOTH

    G in the oval marked "Off the Charts"

    H in the oval marked "Faking It"

    J none of the ovals

5. **Which of the following details belong in the oval marked "BOTH"?**

    A moved to Colorado

    B took classes on the Internet

    C had a sister who is a genius

    D received very high scores on intelligence tests

PROVE THE COMPARISON AND CONTRAST Compare and contrast the two stories by writing a paragraph to support the following topic sentence.

The two stories are alike in some ways, but different in many ways.

_____

_____

_____

_____

_____

_____

_____

VERIFYING EVIDENCE As a reader, it's up to you to weigh the evidence being offered in any piece of writing. When the author has written to inform or persuade, you must verify or confirm the evidence being offered and judge just how believable that evidence is.

Pretend you came across the following item in your daily newspaper. Read the article and then choose the best answer for each question.

[1] Amy Dublowski is making waves wherever she goes. [2] At the age of three she's already a math whiz and reads on a fourth-grade level. [3] Her parents say that Amy's intelligence comes from playing classical music tapes during her mother's pregnancy. [4] Amy's IQ test puts her in the gifted range. [5] Dr. Young, an educator at a school for gifted children, says that Amy is one of the most advanced three year olds he has ever seen. [6] Amy's parents hope she will be in college before she is ten.

1. **Which of the following sentences offers the MOST convincing factual evidence that Amy is truly a gifted child?**
   A Sentence 1
   B Sentence 3
   C Sentence 4
   D Sentence 6

2. **Which of the following sentences offers the LEAST convincing evidence that Amy is truly a gifted child?**
   F Sentence 2
   G Sentence 3
   H Sentence 4
   J Sentence 5

3. **Which of the following sentences offers the reason Amy's parents believe she is gifted?**
   A Sentence 2
   B Sentence 3
   C Sentence 4
   D Sentence 5

JUDGE THE EVIDENCE To persuade the reader of an opinion or story, the author often provides evidence. It is up to the reader to judge if the evidence presented is believable or not.

1. **Which statement offers the best evidence that Michael Kearney is "severely gifted"?**
   A Michael could read at a very early age.
   B Michael was unhappy unless he was learning new information.
   C Michael's sister Maeghan is also setting records.
   D Michael's parents decided to let Michael be Michael.

2. **Which of the following is the MOST likely reason Elizabeth Chapman lied?**
   F She wanted Justin to have opportunities she never had.
   G She was a single mother.
   H She did not have a college degree.
   J She wanted to move to Colorado.

PERSUADE WITH EVIDENCE Write two sentences persuading your reader about something unusual or outstanding about yourself. The first sentence should summarize your story or claim. The second sentence should try to prove that your story or claim is true.

_____

_____

_____

_____

_____

_____

Fatal Mistake

"There's always somebody getting robbed on that corner," said one man. "There's always trouble over there."

The police agreed. One officer said that corner was "like the Wild West."

The place in question was just outside the Boyland Food Center at 373 Marion Street in Brooklyn. Several people had been shot there over the years. Many others had been robbed. So no one was really surprised when two teenagers held up a man on that corner on November 16, 1993. What was surprising was the way the man fought back.

Forty-one-year-old Arthur Boone had worked until midnight. He finished his shift at a local sugar factory and then went to visit a friend. It was almost 3:00 A.M. when he left. On his way home, Boone decided to stop at the Boyland Food Center to make a quick purchase. As he walked back toward his car, two young men ran up to him. Fifteen-year-old Carl James put a gun to Boone's head. "Give it up," James snarled. Meanwhile, 19-year-old Mettaz Pell stood behind Boone and grabbed the wallet from Boone's back pocket.

Boone didn't have a lot of money— just $20 and some credit cards. After taking the wallet, Pell continued to search Boone for money and valuables.

As Arthur Boone stood there, his mind was a tangle of thoughts and his heart was racing wildly. This was not the first time he had been accosted on the streets of New York. He had been mugged six years earlier. During that mugging, Boone had been pistol-whipped so badly he ended up in the hospital. Three years after that, he was robbed again. That time robbers took both his wallet and his car. Now, once again, Boone found himself standing on the street with a gun to his head.

This time, however, Boone had a gun of his own. After the last attack, he had gotten himself a .44 caliber revolver. He carried it with him wherever he went. Even now it was tucked inside his belt, right next to his stomach. Boone feared the teenager who was patting his waist would discover it. If that happened, Boone figured, the young men would kill him.

"I thought I was going to die," Boone later said.

In that moment of panic and anger and fear, Boone saw only one way out. He reached down, grabbed his gun, and fired off three shots. One bullet hit Carl James in the head. Two bullets pierced Mettaz Pell's torso. Pell died right away. James died shortly after being taken to the hospital.

As the two teenagers lay dying, Boone waited for the police to arrive. He told the officers what had happened and why he had used his gun. But when the police checked out Carl James' gun, they were stunned. It wasn't a real pistol. It was just a BB gun—and an unloaded one, at that.

Boone insisted that he hadn't known this. The gun had looked real. The teenagers had seemed dangerous. They had seemed ready and willing to kill him.

"I was fighting for my life," he said.

It turned out that Arthur Boone had no license for his gun. It also turned out that Carl James had never been in trouble with the police before. Mettaz Pell had quite a criminal record. In fact, he had been arrested just two weeks earlier on robbery charges. But Carl James had always steered clear of the police. His mother said he went to school, played the drums and the organ, and never got into trouble. "I don't know what happened; all I know is he got killed," she said.

People all around the city debated what should happen to Arthur Boone. To some, he was a hero who had protected himself in the face of an unprovoked attack. To others, he was a dangerous vigilante who had taken the law into his own hands. When a grand jury heard the case, it decided the truth was somewhere in between. It declined to charge Boone with murder, but it did charge him with three counts of criminal possession of a weapon.

Boone was found guilty of those charges. The judge gave him a light sentence. Boone could have received up to seven years in prison. Instead, he got a $500 fine and five years of probation.

Boone was relieved not to be going to jail, but he said his life had been a "living hell" since the night of the shootings. "I have a lot of sleepless nights," he said. "I have nightmares and a lot of fear." Boone said something else, as well—something that rings true for the many law-abiding people who live in dangerous neighborhoods. Said Boone, "Every day, you take your life in your hands when you walk out the door. It shouldn't be that way."

If you have been timed while reading this article, enter your reading time below. Then turn to the Words-per-Minute Table on page 120 and look up your reading speed (words per minute). Enter your reading speed on the graph on page 121.

Reading Time: Selection 1

_____ : _____
MINUTES   SECONDS

UNDERSTANDING IDEAS Circle the letter of the best answer.

1. **What happened to Arthur Boone outside the grocery store?**

   A He met a friend.

   B He was mugged.

   C He worked until midnight.

   D He made a quick purchase.

2. **What happened as a result of Boone firing his gun?**

   F Boone was sent to prison.

   G Boone was hospitalized.

   H Both of the muggers died.

   J Carl James put a gun to Boone's head.

3. **Why were police surprised when they examined the teenager's gun?**

   A It was a BB gun.

   B It was a .44 caliber revolver.

   C The gun had not been fired.

   D The teens had no license for the gun.

4. **Which statement about Arthur Boone is correct?**

   F He served a short jail term.

   G He had a license for his gun.

   H He was found guilty of manslaughter.

   J He freely told police what had happened.

SUMMARIZE For each blank, choose the word that best completes the meaning of the paragraph.

torso	decided	risk
nightmares	approached	demanded

Arthur Boone was _____ by two teenagers on November 16, 1993. The teens pulled a gun on Boone and _____ money. Boone _____ that if he didn't do something, he might die. Boone shot one teen in the head and one in the _____. Since that night, Boone has had many _____. He says that people who live in dangerous places are always at _____.

IF YOU WERE THERE What would you do if someone threatened you on the street? Write a brief paragraph explaining your actions. Be sure to include examples from the story to support your response.

_____

_____

_____

_____

_____

_____

A Trap in the Woods

Lenny Miller was mad. In fact, he was furious. Three times in eight months someone had broken into his cabin. Some of Lenny's most prized possessions had been stolen or destroyed. And although Lenny had called the police all three times, it didn't look as if the intruder would ever be caught. "I've had enough," declared the 35-year-old Lenny. "The next time he shows up, he's going to be sorry."

Lenny's cabin was deep in the northwest woods of Wisconsin. It was a rustic place—no plumbing, no electricity—but Lenny loved it. He lived and worked in Red Wing, Minnesota, but he and his longtime girlfriend, JoAnn, came to the cabin every chance they got, bringing JoAnn's 12-year-old son Ethan with them. Together they hunted, fished, and rode through the woods in Lenny's all-terrain vehicle. "We're not rolling in money, but this is where we spend our weekends," JoAnn said.

The trouble began in August of 1998. Someone sneaked onto Lenny's property. He or she stole about $1,000 worth of fishing gear out of Lenny's boat. In late January, another incident occurred. This time someone broke into the shed and took Lenny's new chain saw and leaf blower. He or she also broke a window and entered the cabin itself. The thief took almost everything of value. That included three guns. It also included a new knife that Lenny had received as a Christmas present.

The third hit came on Easter morning. Again someone broke into the cabin and took things. The burglar also got into the shed. He or she smashed the ignition of Lenny's all-terrain vehicle.

"That's when Lenny broke down and cried," said JoAnn.

As Lenny put it, "We felt like we were being stalked."

Lenny knew the police were trying. After each break-in, they had checked for fingerprints and tire tracks. But they had no solid leads, and someone was continuing to violate the law. There was a good chance they would never find the person who was tormenting him. So Lenny decided to take matters into his own hands.

He went to a hardware store and bought string, a pulley, and some foam padding. He brought this back to his shed and used it to build a booby-trap. He placed a shotgun under the all-terrain vehicle and attached the gun to the string and pulley. He set it up so the gun would fire at anyone who opened the shed door. Lenny didn't want to hurt an innocent person. So he put a strong new padlock on the door. That way no kid or other innocent explorer would open the shed just to look in. Only a determined thief would make the effort needed to get past the padlock. Lenny also tried to arrange the trap so he wouldn't kill anyone. He aimed the gun low so it would shoot an intruder in the leg, not the heart.

"I just wanted him to get hurt and go to the hospital," Lenny said.

On July 15, Lenny got his wish. A 48-year-old man, Arlin Zuech, sneaked onto Lenny's land. He punched a hole through the shed, tore off the padlock, and swung open the door. The gun went off and blasted Zuech's lower right leg full of buckshot.

Zuech ran off as fast as he could. He was half-collapsed by the side of the road when a police cruiser passed him. The officers saw the blood on Zuech's pant leg. They stopped and asked what had happened. He refused to tell them. Soon, however, an officer remembered the trouble that Lenny Miller had been having. When the police checked Lenny's property, they found the booby-trap and figured out the rest.

Arlin Zuech was arrested and charged with burglary. He claimed he wasn't the one who had broken into Lenny's cabin the other times. Whether or not that was true, he was clearly guilty of this latest break-in. So Zuech, who had a long history of crime, didn't fight the charges. Prosecutors hoped he would go to prison for two years. But the judge surprised them. Judge Edward Brunner sentenced Zuech to five years in prison.

The judge also had some surprises in store for Lenny Miller. It turned out that Lenny, too, had broken the law. In most states it is illegal to use lethal force to protect property. Lenny could have used a gun to save himself, but not to save his belongings. Judge Brunner said Lenny's actions were "taking us back to the days of 'vigilante justice.'" Said the judge, "This is taking us back to the days where there were no rules and everyone carried guns and handled their problems as they saw fit. And that can't be condoned." So Judge Brunner sentenced Lenny to six months in jail.

Lenny wasn't happy about spending time in prison. "What I did was wrong," he said. "But I had to save my sanity and peace of mind." He also said, "I've been asked if I have regrets. No, society's way failed. My way didn't."

If you have been timed while reading this article, enter your reading time below. Then turn to the Words-per-Minute Table on page 120 and look up your reading speed (words per minute). Enter your reading speed on the graph on page 121.

Reading Time: Selection 2

_____ : _____
MINUTES   SECONDS

UNDERSTANDING IDEAS Circle the letter of the best answer.

1. **What did Lenny Miller decide to do the third time he was burglarized?**

   A call the police

   B buy a shotgun

   C set a trap

   D check for fingerprints

2. **Miller took matters into his own hands because**

   F someone he knew was robbing him

   G the police were not trying hard enough

   H the burglar was looking for something particular

   J he didn't believe the police could find the burglar

3. **What did the design of the booby trap say about Miller?**

   A He didn't know how to set the trap.

   B He simply wanted to wound the robber.

   C He did not expect to be robbed again.

   D He was determined to kill the robber.

4. **Which statement would Miller MOST likely make?**

   F "I'll never do it again."

   G "I didn't do anything wrong."

   H "My method worked, and I'm glad it did."

   J "I wish the shot had done more damage."

SUMMARIZE For each blank, choose the word that best completes the meaning of the paragraph.

period	shed	trap
stealing	law	

In 1998, someone broke into Lenny Miller's cabin in the woods, _____ fishing equipment. If that weren't bad enough, someone broke in two more times during an eight-month _____. Miller decided to set a _____ for the burglar. Arlin Zuech got shot in the leg while trying to break into Miller's _____. The only problem for Miller was that he broke the _____ by using lethal force to protect his property.

IF YOU WERE THERE Imagine that you were being robbed frequently. What would you do? Write a brief paragraph explaining your actions. Be sure to include examples from the story to support your response.

_____

_____

_____

_____

_____

_____

_____

USE CONTEXT CLUES When you read, you may find a word whose meaning is unfamiliar to you. When that happens, you can look up the word's meaning in the dictionary. You can also find out what the word means by looking for context clues. These are words or sentences that come before or after the word. Context clues can be words with the same or opposite meanings as the unfamiliar word. They may also be an example or definition of the unfamiliar word.

Read each excerpt from the stories you just read. Circle the letter with the best meaning of the underlined word.

1. **This was not the first time he had been underlined{accosted} on the streets of New York. He had been mugged six years earlier.**

   A accused

   B attacked

   C asked for

   D looked at

2. **To some, he was a hero who had protected himself in the face of an underlined{unprovoked} attack.**

   F unusual

   G strange

   H stressful

   J uninvited

3. **It [the grand jury] underlined{declined} to charge Boone with murder, but it did charge him with three counts of criminal possession of a weapon.**

   A agreed

   B decided

   C refused

   D wanted

4. **It was a underlined{rustic} place—no plumbing, no electricity—but Lenny loved it.**

   F upscale, fancy

   G rusted out

   H interesting

   J country-like, simple

5. **In most states it is illegal to use underlined{lethal} force to protect property. Lenny could have used a gun to save himself, but not just to save his belongings.**

   A deadly

   B firearm

   C gentle

   D strong

PUT WORDS INTO CONTEXT Complete the paragraph using the underlined words from the exercise on this page.

Both Arthur Boone and Lenny Miller were victims of

_____ crimes. Most of the time,

when people are _____, they do

not fight back for fear of what might happen. Both

Boone and Miller _____

to stand still and let criminals have their way. Both used

_____ force to protect

themselves, and both paid the price for it.

MAKE ROOT CONNECTIONS One way of finding out the meaning of a word is by looking for its root. An unfamiliar word may share a common root with a word that you know. A root is a part of many different words and it may or may not be a word by itself. The root *cov* comes from a French word that means "to close or to cover." You will find the root in words like *discover* and *covert*.

Underline the root that connects each group of words. Then choose the best meaning of the root.

1. criminal, crime, criminologist
- **A** misdeed
- **B** accident
- **C** prison
- **D** occurrence

2. probation, prove, probate
- **F** ease
- **G** test
- **H** light
- **J** poke

3. violate, violator, violation
- **A** boast
- **B** disregard
- **C** to play
- **D** purple in color

4. hospital, hostess, hostel
- **F** quickly, late
- **G** sickly, dying
- **H** kidnap, keep
- **J** guest, host

5. force, fort, comfort
- **A** hidden
- **B** lock
- **C** strong
- **D** expensive

6. jury, jurisdiction, juror
- **F** job
- **G** law
- **H** salesman
- **J** medicine

ROOT ANALOGIES Analogies show similar patterns and relationships between words. Root analogies show relationships between words that have the same root word. For example, *use* is to *useable* as *move* is to *moveable*. Both root words, when combined with *able*, make a new word. For each blank, choose one of the boldface words from the exercise on this page to correctly complete the analogy.

1. *Cap* is to *capital* as *hos* is to

_____.

2. *Ter* is to *terror* as *jur* is to

_____.

3. *Derm* is to *dermatologist* as *crim* is to

_____.

4. *Vac* is to *vacation* as *prob* is to

_____.

5. *Oper* is to *operate* as *viol* is to

_____.

ORGANIZE THE FACTS A summary retells the major points of a story. Minor details and examples are not included. To write a summary, first you must decide what the most important points are. You can do this by making a list. Then write a paragraph using the main points from your list. The paragraph is your summary.

Look at the major points listed under "Fatal Mistake." Fill in the missing information. Then list the major points of "A Trap in the Woods."

"Fatal Mistake"
1. Arthur Boone was headed home very late one evening.
2. He was mugged by two teenagers.
3. Boone had a gun and shot the teenagers, killing them both.
4. Boone waited for the police and told them what had happened.
5.

"A Trap in the Woods"
1. Lenny Miller owned a cabin in the woods.
2.
3.
4.
5.

COMPARE THE STORIES Using the major points listed above, write a brief paragraph summarizing "A Trap in the Woods."

_____

_____

_____

_____

_____

_____

_____

FACT AND OPINION A statement of fact is one that you can prove to be true. An opinion is a belief or conclusion that is still open to debate. Read this passage about vigilante justice. Then choose the best answer to each question.

[1] On July 11, 2002, a 15-year-old boy was shot and killed while allegedly trying to steal a bicycle in Baltimore, Maryland. [2] Edward Day, 54 years old, shot the teen in the back. [3] Apparently, the boy was attempting to take the bike from Day's backyard. [4] Police have arrested Day. [5] He is charged with first-degree murder and handgun violations. [6] Day has told police that he slipped on the grass and accidentally fired the gun. [7] Day's neighbors are probably shaken by the incident.

1. **Which sentence from the passage states a fact about what Day's alleged crime is?**

   A Sentence 3

   B Sentence 4

   C Sentence 5

   D Sentence 6

2. **Which sentence from the passage states an opinion about the neighbors' reaction to the crime?**

   F Sentence 4

   G Sentence 5

   H Sentence 6

   J Sentence 7

3. **Which sentences summarize the facts about the alleged crime?**

   A Sentences 1 and 2

   B Sentence 3 and 4

   C Sentence 4 and 5

   D Sentence 5 and 6

JUDGE THE EVIDENCE To convince a reader to agree to an opinion, the writer often provides evidence. The reader has to judge if the evidence is adequate to support the opinion. Choose the best answer to each question.

1. **Which statement best supports the opinion that handling lawbreakers by yourself is not a good idea?**

   A You should let thieves take whatever they want.

   B By hurting a person, you might be breaking a law yourself.

   C You might feel regret after handling a criminal yourself.

   D You should always take the law into your own hands.

2. **Which statement best supports the opinion that Arthur Boone was justified in carrying a gun?**

   F Boone had been mugged twice before.

   G Boone hates convenience stores.

   H Boone might have been a fearful person.

   J Boone was suspicious of all teenagers.

YOUR OPINION Write a brief paragraph expressing your opinion about how to handle people who take the law into their own hands. Support your opinion with evidence from the stories you have read.

_____

_____

_____

_____

_____

_____

The One-Track Mind of a Genius

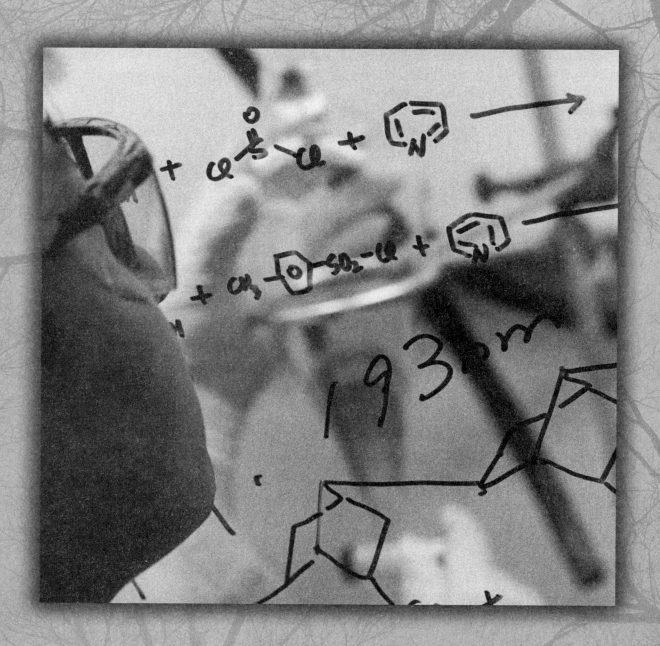

Paul Erdös didn't know how to cook. He couldn't even boil water. He couldn't drive or wash his own underwear, either. Paul Erdös was hopeless when it came to most everyday tasks. Still, he was considered one of the smartest people who ever lived. When he died in 1996, people around the world mourned his passing.

Erdös (pronounced air-dish) was a brilliant mathematician. Even as a young child, he showed tremendous talent. When he was just three years old, he could multiply three-digit numbers in his head.

Paul's parents were math teachers in Budapest, Hungary, and he was their third child. The first two were girls who were said to be even more gifted than Paul was. But his sisters, aged 3 and 5, died of scarlet fever on the day he was born. So Paul grew up as an only child. His mother feared that Paul, too, would get sick and die. So she did not let him go near other children. He was tutored at home until he reached high school.

From his early years, math was Paul's great passion in life. As he once said, "If numbers aren't beautiful, I don't know what is." He paid no attention to the ordinary details of life. He devoted every waking moment to math. As a result, there were many simple things that he didn't know how to do. He didn't learn to tie his shoes until he was 11. He didn't learn how to butter toast until he was 21. Cutting up a grapefruit was something he never mastered, nor did he ever learn to make tea.

As a young man, Paul moved to the United States. Later, he lived for a while in Israel. He was known to mathematicians all over the world. They admired his genius. Most of them freely admitted that he could solve problems they barely understood. One called him "the magician from Budapest." Another dubbed him "the prince of problem solvers." Erdös' biographer, Paul Hoffman, called him "The Man Who Loved Only Numbers."

While most mathematicians slow down by the time they reach their 30s or 40s, Erdös kept going. He worked right through his 50s, 60s, and 70s. He slept only four or five hours a night. The rest of the time he spent doing math. Often he didn't bother to change out of his pajama shirt. He just climbed out of bed and went to work.

In some ways, his life was very strange. Erdös had few possessions. He didn't even have a home. He just traveled around. He went from place to place in 25 different countries. Wherever he went, he carried just two bags with him. One held his clothes. The other held his mathematical papers and notebooks.

When he got to a new place, Erdös headed for the home of the most famous mathematician there. It might be early morning. It might be the middle of the day or late at night. It didn't matter. Erdös would simply walk up to the front door and ring the bell. "My brain is open," he would announce.

For the next few days or weeks, Erdös would work with his host on some mathematical problem. These hosts fed Erdös. They washed his clothes. They took care of him. None of them seemed to mind. They considered it an honor. They loved his sweet, generous nature. More than that, they loved the chance to witness his mind at work. When he got bored, he moved on. But they always hoped he would come back.

One man, Ron Graham, built a special "Erdös room" in his house. Graham also offered to fill out Erdös' tax forms and balance his checkbook. Erdös needed the help. He knew nothing about finances. He gave away most of the lecture fees and prize money he received. Money wasn't math, so it just wasn't important to him.

While many mathematicians guard their work jealously, Erdös shared his ideas with everyone. Paul Hoffman said, "He'd be in a bus and start explaining to the bus driver about the beauty of mathematics. He believed that mathematics was beautiful and elegant,

and he would talk to anyone about it." He even invited other people to write papers with him. He wrote more than 1,500 books and papers in his life. He had more than 400 co-authors.

Erdös had so many friends, colleagues, and co-authors, in fact, that he couldn't always keep them straight. Upon meeting one mathematician, Erdös asked where he was from. The man said he was from Vancouver. "Oh, then you must know my good friend Elliot Mendelson," said Erdös. The man answered, "I am your good friend Elliot Mendelson!"

Paul Erdös never stopped loving numbers and he never slowed down. He finally died of a heart attack at a math conference in Poland at age 83. It was a sad day for everyone. The press noted the death of "the oddball's oddball." But mathematicians knew that Erdös had been more than an oddball. He had been one of the greatest minds of modern times.

If you have been timed while reading this article, enter your reading time below. Then turn to the Words-per-Minute Table on page 120 and look up your reading speed (words per minute). Enter your reading speed on the graph on page 121.

Reading Time: Selection 1

_____ : _____
MINUTES   SECONDS

UNDERSTANDING IDEAS Circle the letter of the best answer.

1. **Paul Erdös was tutored at home until he was old enough to go to high school because**

   A he was afraid of other children

   B his mother did not want him to get sick

   D he lived too far away from the school

   C his mother thought he was too smart for a regular school

2. **Because Erdös spent all his time doing math,**

   F he did not have friends

   G he moved to the United States

   H people thought he was strange and unfriendly

   J there were many simple things he could not do

3. **Which of the following statements is FALSE?**

   A Erdös was born in Hungary.

   B Erdös was called "the prince of problem solvers."

   C Erdös was very secretive about his work.

   D Erdös had no home; he just traveled around.

4. **Which of the following statements would Erdös most likely agree with?**

   F Mathematics is the definition of beauty.

   G I regret not spending time with my family.

   H It is important to have a balance in everything you do.

   J I do not know how I kept up my schedule all those years.

SUMMARIZE For each blank, choose the word that best completes the meaning of the paragraph.

simple	mind	lifetime	constantly
important	unusual	conference	

Paul Erdös lived an _____ life.

None of the things that are usually

_____ to people mattered

to him. All he wanted to do was work

_____ on math. There were many

people who helped him do _____

things like wash his clothes. They did not seem

to _____ helping him. In his

_____, Erdös wrote more than

1,500 books and papers. He died at the age of 83

at a math _____.

IF YOU WERE THERE Imagine what it would be like to be one of Erdös' friends. Write a brief paragraph explaining what a visit from him would be like. Be sure to include examples from the story to support your response.

_____

_____

_____

_____

_____

The Brilliant Oddball

Nikola Tesla had some strange ideas. In fact, some of his ideas were just plain crazy. Tesla was a great scientist. His inventions changed the world. But Tesla was also a dreamer. He tended to go off the deep end from time to time. It was often hard to tell if his thoughts were brilliant or simply bizarre.

Tesla was born in Serbia in 1856. As a boy he spent a lot of time outdoors. Watching birds gave him ideas about flying. So one day he took an umbrella and climbed onto the roof of a barn. Hoping to become airborne, he jumped off. Tesla landed on the ground so hard he was knocked out.

Another time he tried to make a flying machine using June bugs. He glued sixteen of these bugs to some lightweight wood. As he hoped, the bugs beat their wings madly. But to his disappointment, the bugs failed to lift the wood off the ground.

Tesla's inventions soon became more sophisticated. Unlike most inventors, he did not tinker with plans before building an item. He didn't test different designs. He could see in his mind exactly how something would work. So he could build it perfectly the first time. In this way, he invented all sorts of motors.

After moving to America in 1884, Tesla worked for a while with Thomas Edison. He came up with important ideas for using electricity. Tesla's notions laid the groundwork for both radio and television. He developed loudspeakers and the world's first remote-controlled boat. He even foresaw radar systems. In all, he held 700 patents on his inventions.

But while Tesla created many wonderful things, his mind also raced with wild ideas. He thought of building a ring around the earth like a donut. He said people could use this to travel long distances. He talked about building a machine to capture brain waves. He said this would let people read each other's thoughts. He also dreamed up something he called the "death ray." He said it could wipe out ten thousand planes and millions of soldiers in one swift zap.

Perhaps Tesla's wildest moment came in 1899. He was working at a lab in Colorado Springs, Colorado. He wanted to bounce a wave of electricity through the center of the earth to see if it would come back again. So he put on a pair of rubber shoes and sent a huge wave of electricity down into the ground. He hoped the return wave would create a bolt of lightning. It did. In fact, it created the biggest manmade lightning bolt ever. The bolt was 130 feet long. The thunder could be heard 22 miles away.

This lightning was so strong that it blew out all the lights in the city.

Tesla's personal habits were as odd as his ideas. He was terribly afraid of germs. He always washed after shaking someone's hand. He threw away handkerchiefs after using them. Often he did the same with other pieces of clothing. Tesla would eat only from dishes that had been sterilized. Even then, he needed his own supply of napkins. That way he could polish the silverware before using it. If a fly landed on the table, he would not eat his food. A whole new meal had to be cooked for him.

Tesla always calculated the amount of food on his plate. If he didn't, he could not enjoy the meal. He could not stand to touch human hair. He hated the sight of pearl earrings. And he claimed he would get a fever if he so much as glanced at a peach.

Not surprisingly, Tesla had few close friends. His favorite companions were pigeons. Tesla always kept his windows open so these birds could fly in and out. He put food out for them every day. If he was too sick to feed the pigeons, he hired someone to do it for him.

Although Tesla lived to be 86, his health was not very good. As a young man he suffered through a series of illnesses. At times his doctors thought he was dying. Even when Tesla was well, he had strange symptoms. He saw odd flashes of light in his eyes. Random images popped into his head. These images were so strong they were like hallucinations. He wasn't sure what was real and what was not.

There was also a time when Tesla's senses seemed to be too active. He claimed he could feel his bed shaking from the footsteps of people on the street outside his house. He could hear a watch ticking from several rooms away. He could even hear a fly landing on a table.

These sensations finally faded away. But Tesla remained profoundly weird. He always worked with the shades drawn. He slept just two hours a night. At one point he told people he was receiving messages from other planets.

Nikola Tesla was one of the most creative people who ever lived. But he was also one of the strangest.

If you have been timed while reading this article, enter your reading time below. Then turn to the Words-per-Minute Table on page 120 and look up your reading speed (words per minute). Enter your reading speed on the graph on page 121.

Reading Time: Selection 2

_____ : _____
MINUTES   SECONDS

<u>**UNDERSTANDING IDEAS**</u> Circle the letter of the best answer.

1. **How did Nikola Tesla come up with ideas about flying?**

   A by dreaming

   B by watching birds

   C by using an umbrella

   D by spending time outdoors

2. **Unlike most inventors, Tesla could build his inventions**

   F perfectly the first time

   G after testing them thoroughly

   H by going through several stages

   J while studying detailed blueprints

3. **Which of the following statements provides evidence that some of Tesla's ideas were crazy?**

   A Tesla built a remote-controlled boat.

   B Tesla held 700 patents on his inventions.

   C Tesla wanted to build a donut-shaped ring around the earth.

   D Tesla worked with Thomas Edison.

4. **Which of the following statements is FALSE?**

   F Tesla's best friends were pigeons.

   G Tesla hated the sight of pearl earrings.

   H Tesla's ideas were important to the invention of radio and TV.

   J Despite having many illnesses when young, Tesla was always in good health.

SUMMARIZE For each blank, choose the word that best completes the meaning of the paragraph.

suffered	brilliant	death ray	happen
afraid	fly	silverware	ideas

Nikola Tesla was _____, but he

was also very strange. He was _____

of germs and would polish his _____

before using it. Some of his _____

were very important, and others, like the

_____, were simply wild. Tesla

also _____ from poor health much of

his life. Even when he wasn't sick, odd things would

_____. For example, he said he could

hear a _____ land on a table.

IF YOU WERE THERE Do you know anyone who is very smart, but also very odd? Write a brief paragraph comparing him or her to Tesla. Be sure to include examples from the story to support your response.

_____

_____

_____

_____

_____

_____

_____

MULTIPLE MEANINGS Often, words have more than one meaning. When you read a word with multiple meanings, you can look for clues from the words surrounding the multiple-meaning word to determine what the correct definition is.

Use the dictionary entries below to choose the correct meaning of the underlined word.

> **guard:** *n* **1.** one assigned to protect; **2.** a piece of protective body armor; **3.** a decorative trim or lace to protect the edge of a garment; *v* **4.** to protect from danger
>
> **place:** *v* **1.** to put or set in a particular position; **2.** to appoint to a position or job; *n* **3.** physical environment, space; **4.** employment, job
>
> **strange:** *adj* **1.** not before known, heard, or seen; **2.** lacking skill, experience, or knowledge; **3.** characteristic of another country, foreign; **4.** reserved or distant
>
> **wild:** *adj* **1.** not tame (as in animals) **2.** uncultivated region of land, wilderness; **3.** not subject to restrain or regulation, uncontrolled; **4.** barbaric

1. **While many mathematicians guard their work jealously, Erdös shared his ideas with everyone.**
   A Meaning 1
   B Meaning 2
   C Meaning 3
   D Meaning 4

2. **When he got to a new place, Erdös headed for the home of the most famous mathematician there.**
   F Meaning 1
   G Meaning 2
   H Meaning 3
   J Meaning 4

3. **Nikola Tesla had some strange ideas. . . . It was often hard to tell if his thoughts were brilliant or simply bizarre.**
   A Meaning 1
   B Meaning 2
   C Meaning 3
   D Meaning 4

4. **But while Tesla created many wonderful things, his mind also raced with wild ideas. He thought about building a ring around the earth like a donut.**
   F Meaning 1
   G Meaning 2
   H Meaning 3
   J Meaning 4

PUT WORDS INTO CONTEXT Complete the paragraph using the underlined words from the exercise on this page.

Sometimes the world's most amazing people are also

very _____. For example, Erdös

didn't even have a _____

to call home. Nikola Tesla was another odd but amazing

individual. One of his _____ ideas

was to build a machine that would allow people to read

each other's minds.

SUFFIXES A suffix is one or more letters added to the end of a word to change its meaning. For example, the suffix *–dom* means "a state of being." So, when you add the suffix *–dom* to the end of the word *free*, you get *freedom*, which means "the state of being free."

Use a dictionary to find the meaning of each suffix below. Match the suffix with its meaning on the right. Examples for each definition are included in italics. Write the letter of the correct definition on the line. **One of the definitions will be used twice.**

_____	**1.** -ly	**A** action or process: *treatment*
_____	**2.** -est	**B** one skilled in or specializing in: *electrician*
_____	**3.** -ian	**C** state or condition, result of an act or process: *devotion*
_____	**4.** -ion	**D** in the manner of: *quickly, magical*
_____	**5.** -ical	**E** without: *motionless*
_____	**6.** -ous	**F** most (level of comparison): *coldest*
_____	**7.** -less	**G** full of, abounding in: *joyous*
_____	**8.** -ment	

WRITE DEFINITIONS Underline the suffix, and write the meaning of the word on the line provided.

1. mathematician

definition: _____

2. hopeless

definition: _____

3. generous

definition: _____

4. possession

definition: _____

5. mathematical

definition: _____

6. disappointment

definition: _____

7. freely

definition: _____

8. smartest

definition: _____

ORGANIZE IDEAS The main ideas in a story are the larger, more general topics that are covered. The specific details are the facts that clarify or support the main ideas. Fill in the chart by using the items listed at the right. If the bulleted item is a main idea from the story, write it in the row marked "Main Idea." If the item is a detail that supports the main idea, write it in the row marked "Detail."

"The One-Track Mind of a Genius"
Main Idea:
Detail:
Detail:
Detail:
Detail:

"The Brilliant Oddball"
Main Idea:
Detail:
Detail:
Detail:
Detail:

- He was called "The Man Who Loved Only Numbers."

- Nikola Tesla was incredibly creative, but also incredibly weird.

- He believed that mathematics was both beautiful and elegant.

- He had a terrible fear of germs.

- His research helped lay the foundation for the invention of the TV.

- He was tutored at home until he was a teenager.

- He had few close friends, preferring pigeons to people.

- Paul Erdös is one of the greatest mathematicians who ever lived.

- He created the largest man-made lightning bolt ever.

- He didn't know how to do simple things like making a cup of tea.

SUPPORT THE MAIN IDEA Write a paragraph about brilliant people who are also a little strange. State the main idea in the first sentence. Then use details from both stories to support your main idea.

_____

_____

_____

_____

_____

_____

_____

MAKE INFERENCES An author doesn't always state an idea directly in a passage, but you can determine what it is by applying your own knowledge and experiences. You can also examine the evidence presented in the text. This is called making an inference. Circle the letter of the best answer.

1. **What can the reader infer from the following?**

> Paul Erdös was hopeless when it came to most everyday tasks. Still, he was considered one of the smartest people who ever lived.

  A Many people felt sorry for Erdös.

  B Erdös wasn't really as smart as people thought.

  C Most people who couldn't do simple tasks wouldn't be considered smart, but Erdös was.

  D Erdös could not be considered smart because he was dependent on others to get by in life.

2. **What can the reader infer from this sentence?**

> One man, Ron Graham, built a special "Erdös room" in his house.

  F Graham hoped Erdös would return often.

  G Graham was offended by Erdös' strange ways.

  H Graham was a member of Erdös' extended family.

  J Graham didn't want Erdös to visit.

3. **Which is the best inference a reader can make about this sentence?**

> While many mathematicians guard their work jealously, Erdös shared his ideas with everyone.

  A Erdös didn't want to work with other mathematicians.

  B Erdös was so excited about his work that he couldn't help but tell people about it.

  C Erdös bragged about his accomplishments.

  D Erdös wanted people to know which ideas were his.

APPLY WHAT YOU KNOW

1. **What do you think the author intended to do in the first paragraph of "The Brilliant Oddball"?**

  A Criticize the main character.

  B Set up an unusual comparison.

  C Make the reader suspicious of the main character.

  D Give biographical information about Tesla.

2. **Which statement could you infer after reading about Paul Erdös and Nikola Tesla?**

  F Brilliant and creative people can be strange.

  G Building a ring around the earth is a very good idea.

  H Most mathematicians and scientists guard their work jealously.

  J Intelligent people spend most of their time thinking about how to make tea.

JUDGE THE EVIDENCE Based on what you have read from both stories, do you think people who are truly brilliant are also very unusual? Write a brief paragraph explaining your ideas. Support your opinions with evidence from the stories you have read.

_____

_____

_____

_____

_____

_____

_____

SELECTION 1

The Real Dracula

High in the mountains of Transylvania stand the ruins of an old castle. Hidden in mist, it can be reached only after a long climb. Much of this castle has crumbled or been destroyed by earthquakes. But 500 years ago it boasted beautiful rooms, a great dining hall, and strong walls. At that time, it was home to one of the most brutal characters in all of history. The man who lived there was Prince Vlad IV. But today he is most often remembered as Dracula.

Vlad was born in 1431 and died in 1476. He was called "Dracula" because his father's name was Dracul. But the name fit him for another reason, too. "Dracula" means "son of the devil" or "son of the dragon." That was a good description of Vlad. He ruled only six years, but he left a deep mark on what is now Romania.

Some say he was a good ruler. During his rule, he did fight to keep the Turks from taking over his country. He also strengthened the army and built up trade. But the way he treated his enemies was so horrific that most people considered him a monster.

Vlad's favorite form of punishment was impaling, or piercing people's bodies with a sharp stake. In fact, he was known as "Vlad Tepes," which means "Vlad the Impaler." Some say he impaled 40,000 people. Others say it was closer to 100,000. In any case, he condemned a staggering number of people to this slow and agonizing kind of death.

Vlad's targets were often rich landowners in his own country. Vlad didn't trust these people. He knew they threatened his position of power. He also knew that some of them had double-crossed his father. So he looked for opportunities to kill them. On Easter Sunday in 1459, he held a huge feast. At the end of the day, he had his army round up many of the wealthiest guests and impale them. For months their bodies hung on stakes outside his castle.

Often Vlad had the bodies of his victims arranged in what he considered to be artistic patterns. He liked to have the stakes placed in a series of circles. The most important victims were put on the highest stakes. Vlad also liked to vary the position of the bodies. He liked some to hang right side up and others to hang upside down.

Vlad didn't need much encouragement to kill people. He impaled anyone who lied, cheated, or stole. But he also killed people for much smaller offenses. One man lost his life because he ate a piece of Vlad's bread. Another was killed when he gave the wrong answer to a question. On one occasion, Vlad saw a man working in the field. The prince thought the man's shirt seemed too short. Vlad sent for the man's wife and asked her how she spent her days. "I wash, bake, and spin," she answered. This answer displeased Vlad. He decided she had no good excuse for letting her husband wear the wrong size shirt, so he ordered his troops to impale her.

One day a visitor to Vlad's castle was appalled by the carnage. The lawn was like a forest—only with stakes instead of trees. On each stake was a corpse. The odor was so strong that the visitor held his nose. Vlad asked the man if he disliked the smell. "Yes," the man admitted. Vlad then called for a new stake, taller than all the others. He impaled the visitor on this new stake, telling him that at least now he would be up above the smell.

It was bad enough that Vlad killed so many people. But what made it worse was that he took such delight in doing it. During his reign, he devised new forms of torture to go along with the impaling. He often set up banquet tables near the execution sites. That way he could dine while watching his victims die. Some say he enjoyed dipping his bread in the victims' blood.

It was this sort of twisted behavior that made Vlad infamous. After his death, stories about him grew. People claimed he was not really dead. They said he wandered the countryside at night trying to drink people's blood. They said the only way to kill him was to drive a stake through his heart.

In 1897 a man named Bram Stoker wrote a book called *Dracula*. It revived all the old stories. The idea that Dracula was "undead" got another boost in the 1930s. Researchers opened Vlad's tomb—and it was empty. Dracula's body was not there.

If you have been timed while reading this article, enter your reading time below. Then turn to the Words-per-Minute Table on page 120 and look up your reading speed (words per minute). Enter your reading speed on the graph on page 121.

Reading Time: Selection 1

_____ : _____
MINUTES   SECONDS

UNDERSTANDING IDEAS Circle the letter of the best answer.

1. **Prince Vlad IV was known as "Vlad Tepes" because**

   A his favorite form of punishment was impaling

   B he kept the Turks from taking over his country

   C he is most often remembered as the real Dracula

   D he killed people for giving him the wrong answer

2. **Which of the following statements is FALSE?**

   F Vlad built up trade while he was ruler.

   G Vlad took no delight in his murderous ways.

   H Vlad killed people who had double-crossed his father.

   J Vlad had bodies of his victims arranged in artistic patterns.

3. **Vlad often murdered the wealthy landowners in his region because**

   A they lied and stole from him

   B they had cheated Vlad's father

   C he felt they threatened his power

   D they made bad business decisions

4. **What conclusion can the reader make based on the description of how Vlad killed the woman whose husband wore a shirt that didn't fit?**

   F Vlad killed more women than men.

   G Vlad did not want any of his subjects to look sloppy.

   H Vlad wanted to defend his region against the Turks.

   J Vlad would have someone impaled for any reason he chose.

SUMMARIZE For each blank, choose the word that best completes the meaning of the paragraph.

ruler	agonizing	
impaling	reputation	dined

Vlad IV had a _____ for

being a monster. The few good things he did as

_____ are not remembered like

the many horrible things he did. Vlad, who was called

Dracula, killed people by _____

them, or piercing their bodies with sharp stakes. Then he

would let them hang on the stake while they died a slow,

_____ death. Vlad sometimes

_____ while watching his

victims die.

IF YOU WERE THERE Imagine that you lived in Vlad's kingdom. What would it be like? Write a brief paragraph explaining your thoughts. Be sure to include examples from the story to support your response.

_____

_____

_____

_____

_____

The Evil Countess

Everyone agreed that Elizabeth Bathory was beautiful. She was smart, too. But even as a child, she was hard to control.

Elizabeth grew up in Slovakia during the sixteenth century. Her family had a great deal of money. They also had lots of important connections. In fact, Elizabeth's cousin was the king of Poland. Still, the Bathorys were at a loss when dealing with their daughter. She sometimes threw terrible fits during which she behaved like a wild woman. The seizures always passed. But they made everyone nervous. The Bathorys must have been relieved when they could send Elizabeth off to be married.

Elizabeth's husband was Ferenc Nadasdy. She married him in 1575 when she was just fifteen years old. Ferenc was a count, so Elizabeth became a countess. But she was a lonely countess. Ferenc was a soldier. He went off with the army for months at a time. Elizabeth stayed home and took charge of the castle. Part of her job was to discipline the servants. And that, according to legend, was where the trouble began.

Elizabeth decided it wasn't enough just to scold servant girls for mistakes. She came up with punishments that were cruel and painful. She stuck pins under the girls' fingernails. She made them stand in the snow while she poured ice-cold water on them. This went on for years. Elizabeth got away with it because her servants came from peasant families. They didn't dare speak out against a rich countess. Elizabeth's husband didn't help matters any. He didn't seem to mind his wife's mean streak. He even helped her think up new ways to punish the servants.

But if things were bad when Count Nadasdy was around, they got worse after he died. His death in 1604 left Elizabeth at loose ends. She moved to a new castle. It was called Castle Cachtice. Here Elizabeth came completely unhinged. By this time she was getting old. Her beauty was starting to fade. Maybe that's what pushed her over the edge.

One day a servant girl was combing Elizabeth's hair. The girl pulled too hard on a strand of hair. Angry, Elizabeth slapped her. She hit the girl so hard that she broke the skin on the girl's cheek, causing her to bleed. Some of this blood splashed on Elizabeth's face. Elizabeth wiped it off with her hand. But after she did so, she looked at her hand. She thought it seemed different. The part that had touched the girl's blood looked soft and smooth. To Elizabeth's warped mind, it seemed that she had found a great secret. She believed that the blood of young girls could keep her from growing old.

From then on, Elizabeth wanted a steady supply of this blood. She wanted to take baths in it. To get enough, she had to kill her victims. So Elizabeth began a series of murders. She made up excuses to put her servants to death. And for a while, all her schemes succeeded. Twenty servant girls died at her hands. Soon that number had climbed to forty, then to one hundred. In time it rose to six hundred. But then Elizabeth began to run out of victims. Rumors were flying about all the servants who had died at her castle. Few girls wanted to work for her anymore.

At that point, Elizabeth turned to Erzsi Majorova for help. Erzsi was a peasant woman. Her husband was dead. Her future did not look bright. She was happy to become Elizabeth's partner in crime. But Erzsi didn't understand the rules of the game. She didn't know that only poor girls could be killed without causing trouble. When Elizabeth needed new victims, Erzsi urged her to go after girls from wealthy families. Elizabeth did so. And that proved to be her downfall.

These wealthy families did not fear Elizabeth. They wanted revenge. They made sure that the leaders of the land heard what was happening. The leaders decided that Elizabeth had to be stopped. On December 29, 1610, they arrested her. In her room, they found a list of 650 girls. Elizabeth had written the list herself. It gave the name of each one of her victims.

Guards took Elizabeth to a room in her own castle. The room had no windows and just a few small openings for food and air. They locked her in this room and told her she could never leave. She was kept in this one room until her death four years later.

During Elizabeth's life, people didn't think of her as a vampire. After all, vampires are not real. They are make-believe creatures who drink blood in order to stay alive. Elizabeth did not drink her victims' blood. Still, her story was very creepy. As time passed, people did begin to call her a vampire. They made movies and wrote books about her. Today she is remembered as a vampire every bit as horrible as Dracula.

If you have been timed while reading this article, enter your reading time below. Then turn to the Words-per-Minute Table on page 120 and look up your reading speed (words per minute). Enter your reading speed on the graph on page 121.

Reading Time: Selection 2

_____ : _____
MINUTES   SECONDS

UNDERSTANDING IDEAS Circle the letter of the best answer.

1. **How did Elizabeth Bathory's husband react to her treatment of servants?**

   A He didn't seem to mind.

   B He took away her authority.

   C He never knew what she did when he was gone.

   D He scolded her, telling her even peasants are useful.

2. **When did Elizabeth's behavior become dramatically worse?**

   F when she had seizures

   G before marrying the count

   H after the count died

   J when she married the count

3. **What did Elizabeth think would keep her young and beautiful?**

   A drinking blood

   B bathing in blood

   C killing young girls to steal their youth

   D staying out of the sun

4. **What is the most likely reason that Elizabeth's partner, Erzsi Majorova, encouraged Elizabeth to target wealthy families?**

   F Erzsi herself was from the peasant class.

   G Erzsi did not have a future without Elizabeth.

   H Erzsi thought she and Elizabeth could make money.

   J There were no more servant girls and Erzsi didn't know wealthy families would seek revenge.

SUMMARIZE For each blank, choose the word that best completes the meaning of the paragraph.

control	beautiful	treated
reasons	confined	arrested

Elizabeth Bathory was a smart,

_____ woman. The problem was that

she was often completely out of _____.

Elizabeth became known for the terrible way she

_____ her servants. She would make

up _____ to kill the young women.

Eventually, she was _____ and

_____ to a room in her castle for the

rest of her life.

IF YOU WERE THERE Do you know anyone who takes advantage of his or her position? Write a brief paragraph comparing Elizabeth Bathory to someone you know who abuses power. Be sure to include examples from the story to support your response.

_____

_____

_____

_____

_____

USE CONTEXT CLUES When you read, you may find a word whose meaning is unfamiliar to you. When that happens, you can look up the word's meaning in the dictionary. You can also find out what the word means by looking for context clues. These are words or sentences that come before or after the word. Context clues can be words with the same or opposite meanings as the unfamiliar word. They may also be an example or definition of the unfamiliar word.

Read each excerpt from the stories you just read. Circle the letter with the best meaning of the underlined word.

1. **Some say he impaled 40,000 people. Others say it was closer to 100,000. In any case, he condemned a <u>staggering</u> number of people to this slow and agonizing kind of death.**

   A astonishing

   B unsteady

   C arrangement

   D small

2. **The lawn was like a forest—only with stakes instead of trees. One day a visitor to Vlad's castle was appalled by the <u>carnage</u>.**

   F stakes

   G banquet table

   H slaughter

   J weather

3. **It was this sort of twisted behavior that made Vlad <u>infamous</u>. After his death, stories about him grew.**

   A very famous

   B interesting

   C worst possible reputation

   D known only to the surrounding regions

4. **Here [Castle Cachtice] Elizabeth came completely <u>unhinged</u>. Her beauty was starting to fade. Maybe that's what pushed her over the edge.**

   F brutal

   G crazy

   H unhappy

   J powerful

5. **To Elizabeth's <u>warped</u> mind, it seemed that she had found a great secret. She believed that the blood of young girls could keep her from growing old.**

   A cold

   B small

   C one-track

   D twisted

PUT WORDS INTO CONTEXT Complete the paragraph using the underlined words from the exercise on this page.

Two of the most _____ rulers of all

time were Vlad IV and Elizabeth Bathory. Both were

responsible for the deaths of a _____

number of people. Both were also called vampires and

suffered from a _____ view of

themselves and the world. Both were so irrational that it

is likely they were mentally _____.

WORDS THAT COMPARE AND CONTRAST One type of context clue likens or contrasts an unfamiliar word to a familiar word or concept. When you see words and phrases such as *alike, different, both, also, in contrast, but,* and *yet*, you can tell that a comparison or contrast of an unfamiliar term will follow.

For numbers 1 through 8, read the complete paragraph. For each numbered blank, refer to the corresponding number at the right. Choose the compare and contrast word that best completes the meaning of the paragraph.

Today Vlad IV and Elizabeth Bathory are

(1) _____ considered vampires

because of their unquenchable thirst for human blood.

(2) _____ , as you know,

vampires aren't real. The terrible pair were

(3) _____ in that they were each

responsible for the deaths of an unbelievable number of

people. They were very (4) _____

though, in the numbers of deaths each caused. Bathory

killed 650 young girls (5) _____ Vlad IV

killed between 40,000 and 100,000 people. Most people

would (6) _____ that Elizabeth Bathory

and Vlad IV were crazy. (7) _____

most rulers, they killed their subjects

(8) _____ protecting them.

1. **A** also
   B same
   C too
   D both

2. **F** Similarly
   G Likewise
   H However
   J Though

3. **A** another
   B alike
   C separate
   D different

4. **F** different
   G however
   H more
   J together

5. **A** for
   B while
   C in spite of
   D in other ways

6. **F** agree
   G contrast
   H differ
   J like

7. **A** Although
   B Likely
   C Similarly
   D Unlike

8. **F** despite
   G instead of
   H in contrast
   J on the other hand

FIND THE PURPOSE Authors write to inform or teach, to persuade or convince, or to entertain. Sometimes there may be more than one purpose for writing. An author might write fictional stories about evil people in order to convince readers to avoid evil. Those same stories might also entertain readers.

Look at the chart below. Then answer the questions.

AUTHOR'S PURPOSE		
to inform (teach)	to persuade (convince)	to entertain (amuse)
• textbook	• editorials	• fictional stories
• newspaper and magazine articles	• advertisements	• poems
• nonfiction stories/books	• position papers (for or against an issue)	• humorous essays, books, or cartoons
• reviews (movies, books, music, and so on)	• lawyer's briefs (arguments)	• anecdotes (personal stories)

1. **"The Real Dracula" is an example of a passage that should appear under which heading?**

   A to inform

   B to persuade

   C to entertain

   D all of the above

2. **If you purchased a comic book with the title *Dracula Lives*, under which heading would it appear on the chart?**

   F to inform

   G to persuade

   H to entertain

   J all of the above

3. **If someone wrote a flyer titled "Stop the Evil Countess," what would the author's purpose have been?**

   A to inform

   B to persuade

   C to entertain

   D all of the above

4. **An author writes a series of vampire mystery novels. Which purpose might the author have?**

   F to inform

   G to entertain

   H to persuade

   J all of the above

WRITE WITH A PURPOSE Write a topic sentence about evil rulers for each of the purposes you have learned.

to inform: _____

_____

to persuade: _____

_____

to entertain: _____

_____

MAKE INFERENCES An inference is what the reader learns from what the writer has written. When you make an inference, you consider the evidence you've read and then decide what the message is. Circle the letter of the best answer.

1. **What can the reader infer about Vlad from the following paragraph?**

> Vlad was called "Dracula" because his father's name was Dracul. But the name fit him for another reason, too. "Dracula" means "son of the devil" or "son of the dragon."

A Vlad's family was famous.

B Vlad was a vampire.

C Vlad was an evil man.

D Vlad was like his father.

2. **What can the reader infer from the following sentences?**

> Often Vlad's targets were rich landowners in his own country. Vlad didn't trust these people. He knew they threatened his position of power.

F Vlad's family did not have money.

G Vlad disliked people who were wealthy.

H Vlad was a champion of the poor in his country.

J Vlad feared his position as ruler was not safe.

APPLY WHAT YOU KNOW

1. **What was the author trying to accomplish in the first paragraph of "The Evil Countess"?**

A to give background information about Elizabeth's family

B to tell the reader Elizabeth was out of control

C to describe an important event

D to describe life in Slovakia

2. **What did the author mean by saying "if things were bad when Count Nadasdy was around, they got worse after he died"?**

F Elizabeth was relieved when he died.

G Count Nadasdy had a warped mind.

H Elizabeth was cruel when he was alive, but when he died she was much worse.

J Now that her husband was dead, Elizabeth could hire Erzsi.

JUDGE THE EVIDENCE Based on what you have read from both stories, whom do you think was the worse criminal—Vlad IV or Elizabeth Bathory? Write a brief paragraph saying what you think and why. Support your opinions with evidence from the stories you have read.

_____

_____

_____

_____

_____

_____

_____

The Missing Link?

Was he a chimpanzee? Or was he a human? Or was he something in between? That's what people wanted to know whenever they saw Oliver. For over twenty years, this strange creature kept people guessing. Scientists wanted to study him. Circus owners wanted to train him. And millions of ordinary people just wanted to get a look at him.

Oliver came to America in the 1970s. He was shipped over from West Africa by the Burger family. Frank and Janet Burger wanted some new chimpanzees for their animal act. So Frank's brother sent them four chimps from the Congo. The Burgers received all four, but only used three in their act. Oliver was the one who didn't work out.

To begin with, he looked different from the other chimps. He had pale eyes instead of the usual dark yellow. His head was smaller, rounder, and less hairy. While other chimps had round ears, Oliver had pointy ones. His lower jaw did not stick out the way other chimps' jaws did. In short, Oliver looked, well—almost human.

And he didn't just look different; he acted different. "He was odd, and the other chimps would have nothing to do with him," Janet Burger said. Oliver didn't care. He didn't want to hang around other chimps, anyway. He seemed to prefer the company of humans.

He behaved more like a person than any other chimp they'd ever seen. He walked upright on two legs. He liked to sit cross-legged in a chair. And he seemed eager to help Janet Burger with her daily activities. "You could send him to do chores," Janet told reporter John MacCormack. "He would take the wheelbarrow and empty the hay and straw from the stalls. And when it was time to feed the dogs, he would get the pans and mix the dog food for me."

At the end of the day, Oliver liked to relax by having a drink and watching TV. He mixed the drink himself. And in the morning, he enjoyed a cup of coffee.

After a few years, the Burgers sold Oliver to a New York City lawyer named Michael Miller. Miller understood that Oliver wasn't like other chimps. He thought he could make money with him. And he was right. He sent Oliver on tour to Japan. People there lined up to see him. By then, everyone was wondering what Oliver really was. Some thought he was a cross between two kinds of chimps. Others thought he was a new kind of chimpanzee altogether. Still others had a more shocking theory. If humans evolved from chimps, Oliver might be what they looked like along the way. In other words, he might be "the missing link."

Then word leaked out that Japanese scientists had tested Oliver. It was reported that he had 47 chromosomes. Humans have 46. Chimps have 48. So people began to think Oliver might be half-man and half-ape. Dr. Gordon Gallup, a professor at the University of New York in Albany, thought so. "I think there is reason to suspect that Oliver may be a human-chimpanzee hybrid," Gallup said. That would mean that one of Oliver's parents was a human, the other a chimp. Gallup even had a special name for this. He said Oliver could be called a "humanzee."

In the late 1970s, Miller sold Oliver to an animal trainer. In fact, for the next ten years, Oliver went from one animal trainer to another. He starred in many side shows. Sometimes he was called "A Freak of Nature." Sometimes he was called the "Mutant Chimp." Sometimes he was "The Man-Beast." Finally, Oliver was sold to a research company. They didn't do experiments on him. But for seven years they kept him in a small cage. Poor Oliver barely had room to move around.

Luckily, Oliver's story has a happy ending. In 1996, he was given to a man named Wally Swett. Swett ran Primarily Primates. This was a kind of retirement home for animals. Swett gave his animals plenty of space. He fed them well. He took care of their medical needs. Soon Oliver grew strong and healthy again.

And Swett didn't stop there. "Oliver is unique, and there's a reason why," he said. "We want to know."

So Swett asked John Ely for help. Ely was a scientist at Trinity University. He ran tests on Oliver. The tests showed that Oliver didn't really have 47 chromosomes. He had 48, just like other chimps. In fact, Ely's tests showed that Oliver had started his life as an ordinary West African chimp. He had been captured as a baby, and his teeth were pulled. That kept him from biting people. But it also changed the shape of his jaw. It made his face look more human. The differences in his eyes, ears, and head shape were just normal variations. Any chimp might have them.

As for Oliver's behavior, that came from training. Oliver was intelligent. He had learned to imitate his human owners. No one was quite sure why he walked on two legs. Perhaps his legs hadn't developed right. Or perhaps this, too, came from watching humans. In any case, Oliver was not the "missing link." But he was one smart chimp.

If you have been timed while reading this article, enter your reading time below. Then turn to the Words-per-Minute Table on page 120 and look up your reading speed (words per minute). Enter your reading speed on the graph on page 121.

Reading Time: Selection 1

_____ : _____
MINUTES   SECONDS

UNDERSTANDING IDEAS Circle the letter of the best answer.

1. **Why didn't Oliver perform with the other chimps?**
   A He could watch TV and drink coffee.
   B He looked and acted differently.
   C He wasn't smart enough.
   D The trainers thought he looked human.

2. **Why did Michael Miller purchase Oliver from the Burgers?**
   F Miller had always been a chimp lover.
   G Miller wanted to perform research on Oliver.
   H Miller wanted to make money with Oliver.
   J Miller thought he could take better care of Oliver.

3. **The possibility that Oliver might be a cross between a human and a chimp**
   A was why he lived at Primarily Primates
   B prompted a search for more chimps like Oliver
   C frightened people, so they stopped going to see him
   D led to rumors that he had 47 chromosomes

4. **What can the reader conclude after the results of John Ely's tests on Oliver?**
   F Oliver is an unusually intelligent chimp.
   G Oliver is more human than chimpanzee.
   H Oliver is proof that man was evolved from chimps.
   J No one really knows where Oliver came from.

SUMMARIZE For each blank, choose the word that best completes the meaning of the paragraph.

display	excellent	look
animal	use	human

Oliver is a West African chimp who came to America to be part of an _____ act. But the Burger family was never able to _____ him. He acted more like a _____ than an animal. After years of being on _____, Oliver was finally given to a man named Wally Swett. Swett took _____ care of Oliver, who was not a "humanzee" after all. He was a chimp that just happened to _____ human.

IF YOU WERE THERE What would you do if you were an animal trainer and you got a chimp like Oliver? Write a brief paragraph explaining your actions. Be sure to include examples from the story to support your response.

_____

_____

_____

_____

The Monkey Man of New Delhi

No one knew where he came from, and no one knew where he might appear next. But each evening, people in New Delhi, India, scanned the shadows looking for him. All through the night they trembled in fear. They knew he might jump out at any moment. And when he did, people would run in panic. Their cries of terror would fill the air. Then everyone would know the Monkey Man had returned.

The Monkey Man made his first appearance on April 5, 2001. A man named Anil Gopal was sleeping on his terrace when suddenly something attacked him. Gopal told the police it was some kind of monkey. Two weeks later, another man was attacked by a similar beast. This man, too, was sleeping on his terrace at the time.

Word of the attacks spread quickly. More and more people reported seeing a mysterious monkey-like creature prowling the streets at night.

"His back was very big," said one witness.

Others were more specific. They described him as four or five feet tall with hair all over his body and sharp metal claws. According to one person, the creature had "flaming red eyes and green lights glowing on its chest."

Over the next few weeks, many reports were filed at area police stations.

One man attributed a leg injury to an attack by the Monkey Man. Another said the cuts on his body came from the monster's sharp claws. Dozens of people said they had escaped harm but had seen the Monkey Man jump high into the air or move at lightning speed. Everyone seemed unnerved by the strength and speed of this evil creature.

On May 14, Monkey Man hysteria reached new heights. That night, in poor neighborhoods throughout New Delhi, people lay down to sleep on rooftops or outdoor terraces. They knew that being outside left them open to attack, but they had no choice. The heat of summer made it unbearable to stay indoors. Many wished they had lights to keep the Monkey Man at bay. But the power supply usually ran short at night, so most of them would have no light until morning.

In the heat and darkness of that night, it didn't take long for the Monkey Man to strike. In one neighborhood after another, shouts went up that the creature had appeared. People rushed to escape. They scrambled to get off their roofs and terraces. "The monkey has come!" screamed one man. Then he jumped off the roof to his death. Others broke bones or bruised muscles as they, too, leaped into the streets. Some people made it to the streets only to be injured by the stampeding crowd.

A 35-year-old maid named Deepali Kumari saw the Monkey Man that night. "It has three buttons on its chest," she reported. "One makes it turn into a monkey, the second gives it extra strength, and the third makes it invisible."

Kumari and her neighbors screamed when they saw the beast. They started running. One woman, who was pregnant, tried to hurry down the stairs. In her panic, she slipped and fell. She died in the chaos of that terrible night.

By morning, fifty different attacks had been reported around the city. "People are in a state of terror," said Police Commissioner Suresh Roy.

The police wanted to catch the Monkey Man—but they weren't sure exactly what they were looking for. Was the Monkey Man an animal? Was he a person dressed up as a monkey? Was there just one Monkey Man or were there several? To help solve the mystery, police offered a reward to anyone who could take the creature's picture.

The next night, a thousand officers marched out to patrol the streets. But still the panic continued. Again, many sightings were reported. And yet another person died trying to run away from the dreaded beast.

On May 18, the case took a scary new twist. The Monkey Man was blamed for two more deaths. This time the deaths did not occur by accident while people fled. Instead, it appeared that the Monkey Man had killed them. In both cases, the victim had deep puncture wounds on his skull. Witnesses saw a shadowy creature at the scene of each crime. Everyone believed it was the Monkey Man.

Meanwhile, the police were busy tracking down every lead. They realized that many of the sightings were hoaxes. So they announced harsh punishments for false reports. People might get six months in jail.

The police quickly arrested 12 people who reported fake sightings. After that, the number of reported sightings dropped sharply. The last one came on May 20. Two days later, the police made an announcement. There was no Monkey Man, they said. "Our investigations have shown that no such creature exists," said police official Ajai Raj Sharma. "It is more a case of rumors gone wild."

The police declared that the murders of May 18th had been carried out by ordinary humans. The injuries blamed on the Monkey Man were also the result of human actions. People just got carried away by fear or excitement. By the end of the summer, the Monkey Man was nothing but a bad memory.

If you have been timed while reading this article, enter your reading time below. Then turn to the Words-per-Minute Table on page 120 and look up your reading speed (words per minute). Enter your reading speed on the graph on page 121.

Reading Time: Selection 2

_____ : _____
MINUTES   SECONDS

UNDERSTANDING IDEAS Circle the letter of the best answer.

1. **What was the result of Anil Gopal's report about being attacked by a Monkey Man?**

   A Gopal was accused of lying.

   B Gopal became very famous.

   C Soon there were many more reports like Gopal's.

   D Someone took a picture of the Monkey Man.

2. **Which word best describes the community's reaction to reports about the Monkey Man?**

   F anger

   G denial

   H disbelief

   J panic

3. **One of the problems police had with catching the Monkey Man was**

   A they didn't have enough officers

   B there was more than one Monkey Man

   C many of the reported sightings were hoaxes

   D there were too many people in New Delhi

4. **Which of the following statements is FALSE?**

   F People died trying to escape the Monkey Man.

   G Some people who made false reports were arrested.

   H Police announced that the Monkey Man had left New Delhi and had gone to another city.

   J Deepali Kumari said the Monkey Man had three buttons on its chest.

SUMMARIZE For each blank, choose the word that best completes the meaning of the paragraph.

humans	frightened	attacked
escape	reported	announced

The people of New Delhi were

_____. A Monkey Man had

_____ a man while he was asleep.

Other people _____ being attacked

by the Monkey Man as well. One man died after jumping

off his roof trying to _____. Finally,

police _____ that the attacks were

carried out by _____, not the

Monkey Man.

IF YOU WERE THERE What would you do if you lived in a city where a rumor went wild? Would you take extra precautions, or would you just ignore it? Write a brief paragraph explaining your actions. Be sure to include examples from the story to support your response.

_____

_____

_____

_____

_____

_____

USE CONTEXT CLUES When you read, you may find a word whose meaning is unfamiliar to you. When that happens, you can look up the word's meaning in the dictionary. You can also find out what the word means by looking for context clues. These are words or sentences that come before or after the word. Context clues can be words with the same or opposite meanings as the unfamiliar word. They may also be an example or definition of the unfamiliar word.

Read each excerpt from the stories you just read. Circle the letter with the best meaning of the underlined word.

1. **Others thought he [Oliver] was a new kind of chimpanzee altogether. Still others had a more shocking theory.**

   A fable

   B form

   C explanation

   D image

2. **"I think there is reason to suspect that Oliver may be a human-chimpanzee hybrid," Gallup said. That would mean that one of Oliver's parents was a human, the other a chimp.**

   F act

   G fake

   H height

   J mix

3. **The differences in his eyes, ears, and head shape were just normal variations.**

   A birthmarks

   B differences

   C markings

   D similarities

4. **She died in the chaos of that terrible night. . . . "People are in a state of terror," said Police Commissioner Suregh Roy.**

   F confusion

   G heat

   H quiet

   J smoke

5. **They realized that many of the sightings were hoaxes. So they announced harsh punishments for false reports.**

   A beliefs

   B events

   C fakes

   D nightmares

PUT WORDS INTO CONTEXT Complete the paragraph using the underlined words from the exercise on this page.

   Although there are endless _____

to the story, many people believed at one time or another

that the humanzee and the Monkey Man were more than

just a _____. Many believed the

stories were true. Later, the tales proved to be

_____, but in the case of the Monkey

Man, while the story was popular, it was the cause of

much _____.

HOMOGRAPHS Homographs are words that are spelled alike but have different meanings. You can determine the meaning of the word by how the word is used in the sentence.

Read the definitions of each word. On the line, write the meaning of the underlined word as it is used in the sentence.

> **saw:** 1. to have seen with the eye
> 2. hand or power tool with a toothed blade

1. **That's what people wanted to know whenever they saw Oliver.**

   _____

2. **Jim used a saw to take the dead branches off the trees.**

   _____

> **upright:** 1. standing
> 2. honest (as in character)

3. **He walked upright on two legs.**

   _____

4. **The people of the town wanted an upright man or woman as their mayor.**

   _____

> **company:** 1. visitors, guests
> 2. a commercial organization

5. **Finally, Oliver was sold to a research company.**

   _____

6. **My company was late for the birthday dinner.**

   _____

> **patrol:** 1. a unit of persons or vehicles employed for observation, security, or combat
> 2. make the rounds or guard an area

7. **The next night, a thousand officers marched out to patrol the streets.**

   _____

8. **The patrol found suspicious footprints outside the basement window.**

   _____

> **signs:** 1. posters, billboards
> 2. clues or traces

9. **They searched the streets for signs of the monster.**

   _____

10. **We put up signs everywhere when the cat ran away.**

    _____

ORGANIZE THE FACTS There are several different ways to organize your writing. In stories like the ones you just read, the sequence, or order, of the events is very important. In the following charts, fill in the next event(s) in the order that they happened.

"The Missing Link?"
1. Frank and Janet Burger receive four chimps from West Africa.
2. Oliver acts human, seeming to prefer the company of people to other chimps.
3. The Burgers sell Oliver to Michael Miller, who wanted to make money with Oliver.
4. Oliver is sold to several different animal trainers and finally ends up at a research company.
5.

"The Monkey Man of New Delhi"
1. April 5, 2001, the Monkey Man attacks Anil Gopal.
2.
3.
4.
5.

PUT DETAILS IN SEQUENCE Choose the best answer.

1. **Where should this information be in the "The Missing Link?" chart?**

   > "I think there is reason to suspect that Oliver may be a human-chimpanzee hybrid."

   A between 1 and 2
   B between 2 and 3
   C between 3 and 4
   D between 4 and 5

2. **Where would you place this information in "The Monkey Man of New Delhi" chart?**

   > The police arrest people who reported fake sightings of the Monkey Man.

   F at the beginning of the list
   G in the middle of the list
   H toward the end of the list
   J nowhere on the chart

VERIFYING EVIDENCE Because a lot of misinformation gets printed, you must verify the accuracy of everything you read. The way to do that is to weigh the evidence presented and decide whether it is trustworthy. Sometimes part of an article may present the correct facts about something, and part of the same article may deliberately mislead you. You have to decide whether to believe all or only parts of the information you've read.

Read the following sentences taken from "The Monkey Man of New Delhi." Choose the best answer for each question.

[1] A 35-year-old maid named Deepali Kumari saw the Monkey Man. [2] "It has three buttons on its chest," she reported. [3] "One makes it turn into a monkey, the second gives it extra strength, and the third makes it invisible." [4] Kumari and her neighbors screamed when they saw the beast. [5] They ran away as fast as they could.

1. **What evidence would best support Kumari's report about the Monkey Man?**

   A hearing the same report from Kumari's 4-year-old son

   B having a picture of the Monkey Man with the three buttons

   C reading a similar account of the Monkey Man in the paper

   D the opinion of a policeman who was on duty that night

2. **Which sentence in the paragraph would be most difficult to verify?**

   F Sentence 1

   G Sentence 2

   H Sentence 4

   J Sentence 5

JUDGE THE EVIDENCE To persuade the reader of an opinion or story, the author often provides evidence. It is up to the reader to judge if the evidence presented is believable or not.

1. **Which of the following would provide the MOST convincing evidence that Oliver was a "humanzee"?**

   A Dr. Gordon Gallup's learned opinion

   B watching Oliver mix himself a drink

   C watching Oliver perform in a side show

   D confirming the results of the chromosome test

2. **Which statement provides the MOST convincing evidence that the Monkey Man was a hoax?**

   F No person was able to take a photograph of the Monkey Man.

   G Several murders and injuries were blamed on the Monkey Man.

   H In one neighborhood after another, shouts went up that the Monkey Man had appeared.

   J Many people reported seeing a mysterious monkey-like creature.

PERSUADE WITH EVIDENCE Write two sentences persuading your reader that there was never enough evidence to believe that there was a Monkey Man. Be sure to include examples from the story to support your answer.

_____

_____

_____

_____

_____

The Ghosts of Gettysburg

Some people smell pipe tobacco. Others hear drums beating. And some see soldiers standing on the battlefield. A few of these encounters are probably made up. But over the years, thousands of people have reported strange happenings on the fields of Gettysburg, Pennsylvania. Are all of these people lying?

Before the Civil War, Gettysburg was a small, peaceful farming town. But in 1863, it became the site of one of the bloodiest Civil War battles. For three days, smoke from rifles filled the air. Bullets and cannonballs tore into the bodies of soldiers. The voices of wounded men rose over the fields.

During the Civil War, most soldiers smoked pipes. The smell of tobacco was everywhere. Today, few people smoke pipes. Yet even when no visitors are smoking, the smell of pipe tobacco often lingers over the battlefield.

Strange noises are another problem. On some nights, people hear the eerie sound of a drummer beating his drum. They hear cannonballs crashing through trees. Sometimes they hear the sound of rifle fire echoing across the fields.

Not long ago, a woman tried to walk through the battlefield at night. "I was suddenly startled by the sound of a rapidly approaching horse," she said. "The galloping was so near that I actually stumbled backwards in anticipation of getting knocked over. I looked up and there was no horse in sight. Yet I continued to hear it galloping away." Later, the woman learned that a Union officer had been shot and killed on his horse in that very spot.

Sounds and smells are spooky enough. But some visitors say they have seen ghosts as well. Lee and Mary Houser saw three. The Housers were walking along a trail when they came upon three soldiers. The soldiers were sitting on a log. "One was writing, one was reading, and the last one was just sitting there," Lee Houser said. The men looked real enough. But there was something strange about them. They were wearing old-fashioned uniforms. And they didn't seem to notice the Housers at all. When Lee and his wife turned away for a moment, the soldiers disappeared. That was when the Housers realized the men were ghosts.

Others have seen ghost soldiers standing watch at the top of a hill. They have seen sharpshooters lying in wait for the enemy. They have seen a soldier looking for his regiment. And they have seen a soldier singing to a dying buddy.

Pat Keachie was in her Gettysburg hotel room when she saw a ghost. The door was locked and Keachie was alone. Yet suddenly she felt someone or something touch her shoulder. Turning on a light, she cried out, "Who are you? You're frightening me."

"I'm very sorry, ma'am," she heard a voice say. "My name is Caleb."

Keachie looked across the room. She couldn't believe it. She reported, "There in the corner was a Civil War soldier, sitting in the rocking chair with a very long rifle across his knees."

Not all ghosts are that easy to see. Many visitors to Gettysburg sense ghosts but don't see them. This often happens in a part of the battlefield known as Devil's Den. Here, Civil War photographer Alexander Gardner took pictures of dead soldiers lying on the ground. To get a better shot, he asked his assistant to move one body. This may have been a bad idea. Some people say the ghost of that soldier has been angry ever since. That would explain why so many cameras won't work in Devil's Den. Visitors report all sorts of odd problems when they try to take snapshots here. Some are pushed or shoved. Some get their hair pulled. And a few say their cameras have been knocked right out of their hands.

What is really going on at Gettysburg? Do the ghosts of dead soldiers truly haunt the place? Are the sights and smells of the battle drifting across time and into the present day? Or is this all in people's minds? Everyone likes a good ghost story, so maybe visitors are looking for reasons to feel scared. But with or without ghosts, visitors to Gettysburg say it is an experience they will never forget.

If you have been timed while reading this article, enter your reading time below. Then turn to the Words-per-Minute Table on page 120 and look up your reading speed (words per minute). Enter your reading speed on the graph on page 121.

Reading Time: Selection 1

_____ : _____
MINUTES   SECONDS

UNDERSTANDING IDEAS Circle the letter of the best answer.

1. **Which of the following is NOT something visitors report after a visit to Gettysburg?**

   A the sound of galloping horses

   B the sound of a marching band

   C the scent of pipe tobacco

   D the sound of cannonballs being fired

2. **How did Lee and Mary Houser know that the three soldiers sitting on a log were ghosts?**

   F They were wearing modern uniforms.

   G They did not seem to notice the Housers at all.

   H They disappeared after the Housers turned away for a moment.

   J They said strange things to the Housers.

3. **Which of the following statements about Gettysburg is FALSE?**

   A Before the Civil War, Gettysburg was a peaceful farming town.

   B During the Civil War, the smell of pipe tobacco was everywhere.

   C The terrible battle at Gettysburg ended almost 150 years ago.

   D Today every visitor at Gettysburg smells, sees, and hears a ghost.

4. **Which of the following is evidence that people may not be lying about their experiences at Gettysburg?**

   F Supernatural experiences are real.

   G Thousands of people have reported strange things.

   H There are odd things reported at other battlefields.

   J The bloodiest battle of the Civil War was at Gettysburg.

SUMMARIZE For each blank, choose the word that best completes the meaning of the paragraph.

camera	drums	picture
smell	ghosts	battlefields

Even though the Battle of Gettysburg ended about

150 years ago, people today say that there are

_____ that haunt the town. Visitors

who tour the _____ say they can

_____ some of the scents that were

present during the battle. Others say that they have heard

_____ beating and horses galloping.

If you try to take a _____ at Devil's

Den, you may find that your _____

is knocked out of your hands.

IF YOU WERE THERE Do you think people are hearing and seeing ghosts at Gettysburg? Write a brief paragraph explaining your position. Be sure to include examples from the story to support your response.

_____

_____

_____

_____

_____

_____

A Haunted Palace

Spooky things were happening in the Hampton Court Palace. Shadowy figures were seen lurking in corners. Doors were swinging open and shut at random. Loud, anguished screams could be heard echoing through the hallway. No one knew for sure what was going on, but many people had a guess. They said the ghost of Catherine Howard had come back to haunt the palace.

Catherine Howard was born in England in 1522. She was just 19 when she married King Henry VIII. By then Henry was 49 years old and had been married four times. He and Catherine had a few happy months in London's Hampton Court Palace. But soon Catherine became bored. She began spending time with other men. Henry was furious. When he heard rumors that she had fallen in love with someone else, he had her arrested. He announced that he was going to have her head cut off.

Catherine was terrified. She ran screaming through a gallery in the palace. She cried out for mercy, but Henry didn't listen. The guards dragged her away, and she was beheaded in February of 1542.

Hundreds of years later, people walking through that gallery noticed odd sensations. Some felt a sudden chill in the air. Others felt dizzy or faint.

"I felt sick when I turned the corner," said one person.

"The hairs on my arms stood up," said another.

Guards often reported feeling a tap on the shoulder. But whenever they turned around, no one was there. Sometimes palace workers heard cries and screams. And a few times they caught glimpses of a woman running past them.

"What I have experienced is doors opening for no apparent reason," said one palace tour guide. "There's no breeze or anything and the door suddenly swings open, and you think, what's that?"

Tourists also had some strange experiences. One woman fainted when she reached a certain spot in the gallery. She woke up wondering who had kicked her. Later, a second tourist fainted in that very spot. She, too, felt as if she had been kicked.

As time passed, this part of the palace came to be known as the "Haunted Gallery." Said a Royal Palace spokesman, "There have been strange happenings in the Haunted Gallery, there is no doubt about that."

Some said Catherine's ghost was to blame for all the weird incidents. But others thought "ghost" was the wrong term. They argued that the palace was being plagued by a "psychic impression."

A ghost is often defined as a dead person who cannot move on to the world of spirits. He or she is somehow "stuck" among the living. Ghosts may not even know they are dead.

A psychic impression, on the other hand, is different. It is not a person at all. It is just the leftover energy from some traumatic event. Catherine Howard created waves of emotion-charged energy when pleading for her life. Perhaps the palace somehow absorbed this energy. Perhaps bits of it were seeping back out. Like a clip from an old movie, the sounds and images that Catherine had created would then be present again.

In 2000, Dr. Richard Wiseman decided to check out Hampton Court Palace for himself. Wiseman was a famous researcher. He didn't believe in ghosts. He didn't believe in psychic impressions, either. But he was interested in people who did. He wanted to know what these people were experiencing when they went through the palace.

Wiseman brought lots of fancy equipment into the Haunted Gallery. He brought in all kinds of cameras and sensors. For a week he kept track of air temperature. He measured air currents and magnetic fields. He also gathered the impressions of visitors during that time. Wiseman found six "hot spots" in the gallery. These were the places where most of the strange incidents had occurred. After studying these spots carefully, he announced his findings.

"You do, literally, walk into a column of cold air sometimes," he said. But he said it had nothing to do with ghosts. It was because of hidden doors in the palace. Since these doors were not airtight, they created drafts. When people felt the drafts, they were spooked. As Wiseman explained, "If you suddenly feel cold, and you're in a haunted place, that might bring on a sense of fear and a more scary experience."

Wiseman did find one thing he couldn't explain. There was a large green blob on a couple of the pictures he took. But that wasn't enough to make him believe in ghosts. At the same time, his findings failed to change the minds of true believers. They continued to say that Catherine Howard's tragic presence could be seen and felt in the Hampton Court Palace.

If you have been timed while reading this article, enter your reading time below. Then turn to the Words-per-Minute Table on page 120 and look up your reading speed (words per minute). Enter your reading speed on the graph on page 121.

Reading Time: Selection 2

_____ : _____
MINUTES   SECONDS

UNDERSTANDING IDEAS Circle the letter of the best answer.

1. **Catherine Howard was beheaded because Henry VIII**

   A found out that she was a ghost

   B wanted a son she failed to provide

   C thought she fell in love with another man

   D was bored with her after only a few months

2. **"The Haunted Gallery" is the part of the palace where Catherine**

   F was beheaded

   G had her pictures

   H spent time with other men

   J ran screaming before she was killed

3. **A psychic impression is different from a ghost because**

   A it is energy, not a person

   B it appears less often than a ghost

   C people invent psychic impressions in their minds

   D it appears only when people have been murdered

4. **Dr. Wiseman's research at the Hampton Court Palace**

   F did not include interviews with tourists

   G was rushed, and the results were not consistent

   H showed most incidents could be reasonably explained

   J proved that psychic impressions can cause ghostly experiences

SUMMARIZE For each blank, choose the word that best completes the meaning of the paragraph.

| palace | beheaded | sudden |
| fainted | haunted | screaming |

Hundreds of years ago, Henry VIII lived in a

_____ with his fifth wife, Catherine

Howard. Henry had Catherine _____

in 1542 when she was no more than twenty years old.

Today visitors to Hampton Court Palace report feeling a

_____ burst of cold air; others say

they hear _____. A few people have

even _____ in the palace. Is it

coincidence, or is the palace _____

by Catherine Howard's ghost?

IF YOU WERE THERE Do you believe in ghosts or psychic impressions? Write a brief paragraph explaining your thoughts. Be sure to include examples from the story to support your response.

_____

_____

_____

_____

_____

_____

_____

USE CONTEXT CLUES When you read, you may find a word whose meaning is unfamiliar to you. When that happens, you can look up the word's meaning in the dictionary. You can also find out what the word means by looking for context clues. These are words or sentences that come before or after the word. Context clues can be words with the same or opposite meanings as the unfamiliar word. They may also be an example or definition of the unfamiliar word.

Read each excerpt from the stories you just read. Circle the letter with the best meaning of the underlined word.

1. **Today there is no reason why the scent of pipe tobacco should hang in the air. Yet it does. Often visitors catch a sudden whiff of this <u>pungent</u> odor.**

   A strong

   B disgusting

   C light

   D sweet

2. **Yet even when there are no animals in the area, the sound of galloping horses often <u>lingers</u> over the battlefield.**

   F stinks

   G sweeps

   H leaps up

   J remains

3. **Strange noises are another problem. On some nights, people hear the <u>eerie</u> sound of a drummer beating his drum.**

   A beautiful

   B loud

   C creepy

   D faint

4. **Spooky things were happening in the Hampton Court Palace. Shadowy figures were seen <u>lurking</u> in corners.**

   F running into

   G creeping around

   H laughing

   J dancing

5. **It is just the leftover energy from some <u>traumatic</u> event. Catherine Howard created waves of emotion-charged energy when pleading for her life.**

   A upsetting

   B suicidal

   C exciting

   D funny

PUT WORDS INTO CONTEXT Complete the paragraph using the underlined words from the exercise on this page.

Do you sometimes have the _____

feeling that someone is watching you? Is it your

imagination, or are there ghosts _____

about? Visitors to Gettysburg and the Hampton Court

Palace believe that someone or something still

_____ there, even though

the _____ events that occurred in

both places happened many, many years ago.

USING EXACT WORDS Exact words help to create a mental picture in the mind of the reader. For example, which sentence gives you a clearer image? [1] The sky was blue and had clouds in it. [2] The sky was a bright powder blue with airy clouds moving slowly to the east. Unlike sentence 1, which creates only a general image, sentence 2 gives the reader a specific mental picture because it uses colorful adjectives, nouns, and verbs.

Read these sentences and choose the MOST exact descriptive phrase to replace the underlined words.

1. **Others hear <u>drums beating</u>.**
   A soldiers beating drums
   B the beating of the war drums
   C drums pounding loudly
   D the sad beating of the drums of war

2. **A few of these encounters were probably <u>made up</u>.**
   F outright lies
   G fake anyway
   H creations of an imaginative mind
   J more than likely wishful thinking

3. **They have seen a soldier <u>looking</u> for his regiment.**
   A trying to find
   B hoping to come across
   C wondering if he will ever see
   D searching the smoking battlefields

4. **Tourists also had some <u>strange experiences</u>.**
   F weird incidents
   G ghostly encounters
   H odd happenings
   J unexplained feelings

5. **She cried out for mercy, but Henry didn't <u>listen</u>.**
   A lend an ear
   B hear her gut-wrenching pleading
   C notice
   D see clearly

ANALOGIES As you have seen in previous exercises, analogies show relationships and patterns between words. The relationships can be very different things, not just synonyms and antonyms. For example, *hat* is to *head* as *glove* is to *hand*. The first words (*hat* and *glove*) are meant to cover the second words (*head* and *hand*). For each blank, choose an underlined word from the exercise on this page to correctly complete the analogy. In most cases, you will only use one of the underlined words.

1. *Voices* is to *singing* as *drums* is to

   _____ .

2. *Shouting* is to *yelling* as *searching* is to

   _____ .

3. *Mouth* is to *talk* as *ear* is to

   _____ .

4. *Genuine* is to *fake* as *real* is to

   _____ .

5. *Usual* is to *ordinary* as *unusual* is to

   _____ .

PRACTICE SUMMARIZING A summary is a retelling of the main points of a story. Summaries do not attempt to recount every detail. The reason summaries are useful is that they are always shorter than the original piece. For example, if you find a TV guide in the newspaper, there is often a summary of what a show is about. A sentence is usually enough to summarize a half-hour program.

Practice writing one-sentence summaries of these books about ghosts and other supernatural beings. Use only one sentence. You decide what the book will be about based on the title. The first one is done for you.

Book Title and One-sentence Summary

1. *Ghosts of the Alamo*

   Many visitors have seen ghosts of soldiers who

   died at the Alamo.

   _____

2. *Psychic Impressions—Fact or Fiction?*

   _____

   _____

   _____

3. *Is the Governor's Mansion Haunted?*

   _____

   _____

   _____

4. *The Philadelphia Phantom*

   _____

   _____

   _____

SUMMARIZE THE STORIES In the space provided, write a one-paragraph summary of each of the selections. Be sure to include only the main points from each selection.

"The Ghosts of Gettysburg"

_____

_____

_____

_____

_____

_____

_____

"A Haunted Palace"

_____

_____

_____

_____

_____

_____

_____

MAKE PREDICTIONS You can make predictions, or educated guesses, based on what you already know. For example, many people predict what time of day the traffic will be the worst and plan to avoid the highway at that time. Read this passage, and answer the following questions.

Home Sweet Home

The Bell family just moved into a house in Ellicott City's historic district. Local legend says that the original owner of the house used to murder his dinner guests who had no known relatives. Then he would build them into the walls of the house, sealing them in forever. The Bells knew the stories about the house, but felt they were probably all made up. Lately, though, they've begun to wonder. There are strange noises coming from the attic, and Mr. Bell found his softball glove and bat in the storage space under the stairwell. He knows for certain that he put his gear in the hall closet. Everyone is beginning to wonder what is going on.

---

1. **What do you predict Mr. Bell might do next?**

   A Sell the house and move to another city.

   B Investigate the real cause of the strange happenings.

   C Look for the ghosts.

   D Find other haunted houses in Ellicott City.

2. **What do you predict the city's historical society might be able to provide?**

   F no additional information

   G books about ghosts

   H detailed information about the history of the house

   J a reasonable explanation for all the strange noises

3. **Predict what the head of the Ellicott City Ghosts and Goblins Society might say to the Bells.**

   A The Bells should leave the society alone.

   B The Bell house is definitely haunted.

   C The Bells are just trying to get publicity.

   D The Bells are overreacting to the strange noises.

JUDGE THE BASIS OF A PREDICTION For predictions to be reasonably accurate, they must be based on what you know to be factual information. Choose the best answer.

1. **Which new information will help you predict that the Bells will have their home re-inspected?**

   A Mrs. Bell always rearranges things in the house.

   B Mr. Bell likes to entertain guests with ghost stories.

   C They heard strange noises in another house, too.

   D They found a hidden doorway in a closet.

2. **Which new information helps you predict that maybe the Bell house is not really haunted?**

   F The Bell's daughter loves to play practical jokes.

   G The attic is dark and full of cobwebs.

   H Their neighbors saw ghosts in the house.

   J The Ghosts and Goblins Society says the house is haunted.

PREDICT WHAT YOU WOULD DO Write a brief paragraph explaining what you would do if you lived in a house you thought might be haunted. Use examples from the stories you just read to explain your actions.

_____

_____

_____

_____

_____

Maniacs in the Subway

It doesn't happen very often. But when it does, it's terrifying. Imagine standing at the edge of a subway platform, waiting for a train. Now imagine that a train is roaring into the station. Just as it approaches, someone comes up behind you and pushes you onto the tracks in front of it.

That's exactly what happened to Amy Chan. On March 5, 2002, 21-year-old Amy was on her way to school. She entered the Coxwell subway station in Toronto, Canada, and headed for the westbound platform. But as a train rattled toward her, a stranger stepped out of the crowd. The woman shoved Amy from behind, deliberately knocking her into the path of the oncoming train.

"I thought I was dead," Amy said. "It was the scariest day of my life."

Amy was lucky. She managed to crawl off the tracks just as the train barreled past. Shocked commuters reached down and helped her back onto the platform. She had a few cuts and bruises and she was shaking with fear, but otherwise she was unhurt.

Edgar Rivera was less fortunate. Rivera was a 46-year-old father of three. On April 29, 1999, he was in New York City's 51st Street station. It was rush hour, so the station was packed with commuters. Edgar was standing near the edge of the platform, minding his own business. But as a train approached, a stranger suddenly stepped up next to him and gave him a push.

"Oh, my God!" yelled Edgar as he tumbled down onto the tracks.

Edgar had no time to scramble to safety. The best he could do was to kneel against the side of the tunnel and press his face and chest into the concrete. That saved his life. But his legs still stuck out onto the tracks. The train ran over them as it passed into the station.

Everyone who witnessed this terrible scene thought Edgar Rivera was dead. That included Fire Captain Fred Ill, one of the first rescue workers on the scene. "People were reporting to us that he was dead," said Ill. "But when I looked down between the two cars and shined the flashlight down at him, his eyes opened and he looked at me."

Edgar was alive, but he was in shock and losing blood fast. Rescue workers rushed him to the hospital. Doctors stabilized him. They tried to reattach his legs, but couldn't. When Edgar was finally released from the hospital, he was a double amputee.

And then there was Charlene Minkowski. She was a law clerk in Toronto. On September 26, 1997, Charlene had some business in another part of the city. So at 11:00 A.M. she entered the Dundas station. She didn't pay any attention to the strange man who was loitering on the platform nearby. But as a train pulled into the station, this man suddenly sprang forward. He stepped up to Charlene and pushed her. She didn't stand a chance. She lost her balance and fell onto the tracks. She died when the train hit her.

In all three of these cases, the victims just happened to be in the wrong place at the wrong time. They didn't know their attackers. They never had any previous contact with him or her, and they had done nothing to provoke the attack. These were truly random acts of violence.

And there were others. In the 1990s, there were more than a dozen similar cases around the world. Sixty-three-year-old Soon Sin was killed when a man pushed her in front of a subway train in New York. The same fate befell 32-year-old Kendra Webdale. In Paris, a 41-year-old man was lucky to walk away with just a broken arm after a stranger threw him onto the tracks. And in London, a 29-year-old woman lay dazed after a stranger shoved her down. She lived only because the engineer was able to stop the train inches from her body.

Who would do such a terrible thing? Who would push an innocent commuter in front of a moving train? In almost every case, the attacker had a history of violence, drug abuse, and mental illness. Amy Chan's assailant had been to court several times for assaulting people. Edgar Rivera's attacker was a drug user who thought people were trying to kill him. And Charlene Minkowski's killer had been considered mentally ill for years.

It is important to remember that such cases are rare. Millions of people ride the subways safely every day. But it's also a good idea to play it smart. When waiting on a subway platform, never stand close to the edge. "Stay away from the yellow line," advised police spokesman Jim Muscat. "And always be alert and aware of your surroundings."

If you have been timed while reading this article, enter your reading time below. Then turn to the Words-per-Minute Table on page 120 and look up your reading speed (words per minute). Enter your reading speed on the graph on page 121.

Reading Time: Selection 1

_____ : _____
MINUTES   SECONDS

UNDERSTANDING IDEAS Circle the letter of the best answer.

1. **What was the extent of Amy Chan's injuries?**

   A She was killed.

   B Both of her legs were amputated.

   C Her legs were broken.

   D She had cuts and bruises.

2. **How did Edgar Rivera save his own life?**

   F He tucked his knees under his chin.

   G He pressed his chest and face into the side of the tunnel.

   H He crawled off the tracks just in time.

   J He scrambled back up on to the platform before the train passed.

3. **What did all of the victims have in common?**

   A They did not know their attackers.

   C They did not suffer serious injuries.

   B They both had enemies who shoved them from behind.

   D They were both in New York City when they were attacked.

4. **Based on the incidents in the story, which conclusion can a reader draw about the attackers?**

   F They know exactly whom to attack.

   G They all suffer from mental illness.

   H They have been to jail several times.

   J They have no fear of being caught.

SUMMARIZE For each blank, choose the word that best completes the meaning of the paragraph.

pushed	alert	violence
cases	illness	attackers

People like Amy Chan, Edgar Rivera, and Charlene Minkowski have all suffered from unprovoked acts of _____. All were _____ in front of oncoming trains. They are not the only ones, however. During the 1990s, there were more than twelve _____ like Chan's, Rivera's, and Minkowski's. Virtually all of the _____ had symptoms of mental _____. The important thing to remember is to be _____ and watchful when waiting for a train.

IF YOU WERE THERE Write a brief paragraph explaining what you would do if you witnessed an act of violence like the one committed against Amy Chan. How would you react? Be sure to include examples from the story to support your response.

_____

_____

_____

_____

_____

Arson in a Small Town

"The whole town is on edge." That's how John Harrigan put it in the summer of 1988. Harrigan was one of about 900 people who lived in the tiny town of Jefferson, New Hampshire. In the past, people in Jefferson had enjoyed quiet lives. They felt safe. But now everything seemed different. Now there was an arsonist in their midst.

The trouble began on May 5. At 11:00 P.M. that night, a grass fire broke out on Turnpike Road. Because Jefferson is so small, it doesn't have a full-time fire department. Instead, citizens from the town serve as volunteer firefighters. Several of these volunteers rushed to Turnpike Road and put out the blaze.

The next night brought another fire. This time it was a barn on Valley Road. Over the next nine days, five more fires erupted. Three were grass or brush fires. One was another barn. And one was an empty vacation home.

Investigators didn't think any of these fires started on their own. They believed someone had set them. Townspeople shuddered at the news. Still, it seemed that the arsonist—whoever he or she was—was not trying to hurt anyone. Only empty buildings and fields had been targeted.

That changed on May 24. As the sun set that evening, the Skywood Manor Motel burst into flames. Luckily, William Perkins, one of the volunteer firefighters, lived across the street. Perkins happened to be home when the fire started. He used fire extinguishers from the motel to put out the flames. A few of the rooms were damaged, but the building was saved and no one was hurt.

Three days later, things got even creepier. Perkins was getting ready for bed when he heard tires squealing in his driveway. "When I opened the stairway door, the flames just exploded toward me," he later said. He roused his wife and their two children and got them safely out of the house.

After the Perkins fire, it was clear that the arsonist was literally playing with people's lives. And he or she wasn't done yet. June was relatively quiet, with only two fires set that month. Both were in unoccupied buildings. But on the night of July 1, a smoke alarm went off in Bruce and Donna Hartford's house. The family awoke to find their house in flames. They escaped only by scrambling through a second story window. One of the children needed hospital treatment for smoke inhalation. So did one firefighter.

By this time, nighttime had become a nightmare for the people of Jefferson. Many people left their lights on all night or set up bright spotlights in their yards. Some stood guard at doors or windows.

John Harrigan, editor of the local paper, stayed home every night to protect his children and property. On August 5, however, he decided to make an exception. He took his family out to dinner. While they were eating in a nearby town, someone broke into their house and started a fire. Firefighters put out the blaze in time to save most of the house, but Harrigan was shaken by the timing of the attack. Had the arsonist been lying in wait, ready to destroy his house as soon as he left it unguarded? "I hope this doesn't mean that whoever it is has been watching me for a long time," Harrigan said.

Authorities didn't know of any reason why Harrigan would be targeted. But it did seem that the arsonist was familiar with the town and its residents. By this time he or she had managed to set sixteen fires without getting caught.

And more were yet to come. All through August and September, the unknown arsonist terrorized the people of Jefferson. Every few days there was another fire, another homeless family, another brush with death. The town's firefighters were exhausted.

But they were also suspects. "It's a known fact that quite frequently in these situations the arsonist is within the [fire] department," said one firefighter. In several of the Jefferson cases, a firefighter had either been the one to report the fire or had been the target of the arson. The local firefighters knew this and found it hard to keep their spirits up. "When I'm out there battling fires, I hate knowing that people are wondering about me," said one.

It wasn't just the firefighters who were uneasy. Many others felt they were under suspicion. "I look at customers sometimes and wonder if they are the one," said a shopkeeper. "I'm sure they look at me the same way. It's an awful way to live."

Finally, in October, the police made an arrest. The man accused of setting the fires was 23-year-old Lance LaLumiere. LaLumiere, who had learning disabilities and an IQ of just 81, had always struggled unsuccessfully to keep up with his peers. Most people doubted he had the cunning to set 26 fires without being caught.

In the end, the courts agreed. LaLumiere was found not guilty. Most residents applauded the verdict. But that left one big question. If LaLumiere wasn't the arsonist, who was?

After LaLumiere's arrest, no more fires were set. That didn't mean the arsonist was gone. It just meant that he or she hadn't been caught. Somewhere, the person responsible for setting the 26 Jefferson fires is still free.

If you have been timed while reading this article, enter your reading time below. Then turn to the Words-per-Minute Table on page 120 and look up your reading speed (words per minute). Enter your reading speed on the graph on page 121.

Reading Time: Selection 2

_____ : _____
MINUTES   SECONDS

UNDERSTANDING IDEAS Circle the letter of the best answer.

1. **Who put out the grass fire on Turnpike Road?**
   A Lance LaLumiere
   B volunteer firefighters
   C citizens from a nearby town
   D the person who lived across the street

2. **After the Perkins fire, what conclusion could the reader make?**
   F The arsonist was from out of town.
   G The arsonist liked hotel fires best.
   H The arsonist was from the fire department.
   J The arsonist intended to hurt someone.

3. **Based on the story, which of the following is NOT a precaution townspeople took?**
   A People set up video cameras.
   B People left their lights on all night.
   C People installed bright spotlights in their yards.
   D People stood guard at their doors or windows.

4. **What conclusion did most townspeople make about Lance LaLumiere?**
   F LaLumiere was the arsonist.
   G He was too young to be an arsonist.
   H He was not smart enough to have set the fires.
   J LaLumiere was being treated poorly.

SUMMARIZE For each blank, choose the word that best completes the meaning of the paragraph.

not guilty	fearful	fires
volunteer	arsonist	deliberately

Citizens who served as _____ firefighters put out the first fire on May 5. Over the next nine days, five more _____ broke out. The fires were being set _____, but no one knew by whom. The townspeople were _____, thinking that at any moment their homes could be next. Eventually, Lance LaLumiere was arrested for the crimes, but he was found _____. No one knows who the _____ of Jefferson was.

IF YOU WERE THERE Write a brief paragraph explaining what you would do if you were John Harrigan's neighbor the night his house was set on fire. Be sure to include examples from the story to support your response.

_____

_____

_____

_____

_____

USE CONTEXT CLUES When you read, you may find a word whose meaning is unfamiliar to you. When that happens, you can look up the word's meaning in the dictionary. You can also find out what the word means by looking for context clues. These are words or sentences that come before or after the word. Context clues can be words with the same or opposite meanings as the unfamiliar word. They may also be an example or definition of the unfamiliar word.

Read each excerpt from the stories you just read. Circle the letter with the best meaning of the underlined word.

1. **Amy was lucky. She managed to crawl off the tracks just as the train barreled past. Shocked commuters reached down and helped her back onto the platform.**

   A students

   B travelers

   C subway workers

   D police officers

2. **She didn't pay any attention to the strange man who was loitering on the platform nearby. But as the train pulled into the station, this man suddenly sprang forward.**

   F slipping

   G yelling

   H exiting

   J waiting

3. **And in London, a 29-year-old woman lay dazed after a stranger shoved her down. She lived only because the driver of the train was able to stop the train inches from her body.**

   A stunned

   B laughing

   C silent

   D bleeding

4. **Investigators didn't think any of these fires started on their own. They believed someone had set them. Townspeople shuddered at the news. They hated to think anyone would do such a thing.**

   F got angry

   G shook with horror

   H didn't believe

   J laughed it off

5. **John Harrigan, editor of the local paper, stayed home every night to protect his children and property. On August 5, however, he decided to make an exception.**

   A new rule

   B practical joke

   C change from the normal

   D special inspection

PUT WORDS INTO CONTEXT Complete the paragraph using the underlined words from the exercise on this page.

Are you one of the thousands of

_____ who ride the subway

to work every day? If so, be very aware of anyone,

man or woman, who appears to be aimlessly

_____ around the platform before

the train arrives. Several times, attackers have pushed

innocent people into the path of an oncoming train.

Without _____ it seems these

people have a history of violence. The victims and other

onlookers are completely _____

by the evil crime.

SIMILES AND METAPHORS Writers use similes and metaphors to make their writing more vivid. Similes and metaphors are comparisons between words. Similes are easy to spot because they include the words *like* or *as*. Here's an example: *She was poised like a cat ready to pounce.* Here's another simile: *Ira was as cunning as a snake when it came to business deals.* Metaphors are a little different because the comparisons do not use the words *like* or *as*. Here's an example of a metaphor: *The nurse was an angel of mercy.* The sentence means the nurse was very kind to his or her patient.

Read the following sentences. Decide whether the comparison is a simile or metaphor. Write S for simile or M for metaphor in the blank on the left.

_____ **1.** The train roared into the station like a lion.

_____ **2.** The commuters on the subway were as close together as sardines in a can.

_____ **3.** The attackers were demons who tormented innocent people.

_____ **4.** The arsonist was like a snake in the grass, ready to strike at any time.

_____ **5.** Nighttime was a nightmare for the people of Jefferson.

WHAT'S THE COMPARISON? Read the following sentences. In the space provided, write what two things are being compared.

1. The arsonist set the fire and escaped undetected, like a thief in the night.

_____

2. The strange man was a panther who sprang forward and pushed Charlene onto the tracks.

_____

3. Subway attackers are as dangerous as venomous snakes.

_____

4. The arsonist was like a beast of prey, ready to destroy as soon as the victim was off guard.

_____

5. The power of suspicion was a poison ruining many old friendships in Jefferson.

_____

ORGANIZE IDEAS Let's review. The main ideas in a story are the main topics that are discussed. The specific details are the facts that clarify or support the main ideas. Fill in the chart by using the items listed at the right. If the bulleted item is a main idea from the story, write it in the row marked "Main Idea." If the item is a detail that supports the main idea, write it in the row marked "Detail."

"Maniacs in the Subway"
Main Idea:
Detail:
Detail:
Detail:
Detail:

"Arson in a Small Town"
Main Idea:
Detail:
Detail:
Detail:
Detail:

- Kendra Webdale was killed when she was pushed in front of a subway train.

- No one knows who started the 26 fires in Jefferson, New Hampshire.

- Edgar Rivera survived his attack, but both of his legs were severed.

- Bruce and Donna Hartford awoke to find their home on fire.

- At first, the fires were in fields or empty buildings.

- The attackers usually suffer from mental illness.

- Lance LaLumiere was arrested on suspicion of arson.

- Several people have been pushed into the paths of oncoming trains.

- People in Jefferson became suspicious of one another.

- Amy Chan was 21 years old when she was pushed onto the tracks.

SUPPORT THE MAIN IDEA Write a paragraph about random acts of violence. State the main idea in the first sentence. Then use details from both stories to support your main idea.

_____

_____

_____

_____

_____

_____

_____

FACT AND OPINION Facts and opinions can sometimes be hard to tell apart. People often represent an opinion as if it were a fact. To tell if something is a fact or opinion, determine whether what is being said is something that can be proven to be true. If it can, it's a fact. If not, it's someone's opinion.

Read this passage about recognizing mental illness. Then choose the best answer to each question.

[1] Random violence on subway platforms can be prevented. [2] If the attackers suffer from mental illness, they should be stopped by family members who know how to recognize the signs. [3] Someone who is always hostile, suspicious, and fearful is a likely candidate. [4] Other symptoms include alternating periods of hyperactivity and inactivity, social withdrawal, isolation, and indifference. [5] Anyone with a history of mental illness who displays these symptoms should not be allowed on a subway platform.

1. **Which sentence from the paragraph states a FACT about what the symptoms of mental illness are?**

   A Sentence 1

   B Sentence 2

   C Sentence 4

   D Sentence 5

2. **Which sentence from the paragraph states an OPINION about a mentally ill person's family?**

   F Sentence 1

   G Sentence 2

   H Sentence 3

   J Sentence 4

3. **Which sentence from the paragraph most clearly states the author's opinion about mental illness and subway violence?**

   A Sentence 2

   B Sentence 3

   C Sentence 4

   D Sentence 5

JUDGE THE EVIDENCE Think back to what you have read. Review the paragraph about mental illness at the left. Then choose the best answer.

1. **Which of the following statements is TRUE?**

   A A person who is always indifferent is mentally ill.

   B Subway platforms are full of mentally ill people.

   C Family members can learn to recognize signs of mental illness.

   D A mentally ill person always attacks innocent commuters.

2. **Which of the following statements is FALSE?**

   F Someone who suddenly becomes hostile might be mentally ill.

   G Each subway platform has at least one dangerous, mentally ill person on it.

   H Suspicion and fearfulness are among many symptoms of mental illness.

   J Alternating periods of hyperactivity and inactivity may indicate mental illness.

YOUR OPINION Write a brief paragraph expressing your opinion about how random violence can be prevented. Support your opinion with evidence from the stories you have read.

_____

_____

_____

_____

_____

_____

_____

_____

The Perfect Spy

No one suspected a thing. Everyone thought George Trofimoff was completely trustworthy. After all, he was a colonel in the United States Army. He had spent his entire career working for America. No one had any idea that he was really a traitor, but he was. For 25 years, George Trofimoff sold military secrets to the Russians.

Trofimoff began working with the Russians around 1969. In some ways, it was a natural thing for him to do. After all, his parents were Russian. He had been born in Germany, but his parents still thought of Russia as their homeland. George's mother died when he was a baby. So he was raised by the Susemihl family. They, too, were Russians living in Germany. They, too, remembered Russia as the "motherland."

George was close to the Susemihls' son Igor. The two boys were like brothers. They were separated when George moved to America. Igor stayed in Germany and went on to become a high-ranking priest in the Russian Orthodox Church. But he and George never lost touch with each other. And Igor was to play an important role in George's later life.

In America, George worked hard to be a success. He became an American citizen. He joined the Army Reserves. And he went to work as an intelligence officer.

In time, he rose to a position of great power. He was put in charge of a special office in Germany. It was a place where Russian defectors were interviewed. The defectors knew a lot of secrets about Russia's government. George and his team kept track of this information.

Meanwhile, George was still in contact with Igor. One day Igor came to him with a bold plan. We will never know exactly what Igor said. Maybe he asked for a favor. Maybe he told George that "Mother Russia" needed him. Or maybe he just offered George money. In any case, George agreed to the plan. He said he would switch sides. He would become a spy for Russia.

George was in a perfect position to do this. Everyone trusted him. Everyone viewed him as a patriotic American. Also, he was the top man in the office. So none of his colleagues asked questions if they saw him looking through secret papers. He could easily get his hands on every document in the building.

Slowly George began to gather information for the Russians. He sneaked papers home. He photographed them and then returned them to the office. He passed the photos on to Igor, who turned them over to the Russians. In all, George gave about 50,000 pages of top-secret documents to the Russians. No one questioned why he had so many meetings with Igor. Everyone knew they were old friends. Everyone knew they thought of themselves as brothers.

For years George spied for the enemy and got away with it. As one American later put it, he did a very good job. "George Trofimoff wasn't an accidental spy," said Laura Ingersoll. "He wasn't casual and he wasn't a sloppy spy. In a very real sense he was the perfect spy."

But in 1992, George's "perfect" situation began to unravel. A Russian named Vasili Mitrokhin defected to the American side. Mitrokhin brought disturbing news with him. He said an American officer was passing secrets to a Russian priest.

American officials sat down and tried to figure out who it could be. They took a look at anyone with connections to a Russian priest. George was the obvious suspect.

By this time, George was about to retire. In 1994, he left the army and moved to Florida. There he lived a quiet life in a quiet community. He made a little pocket money by bagging groceries at a local store. Other than that, he kept to himself.

American agents were still on his trail, however. They wanted to know if he really had been helping the Russians.

In 1997, these agents set a trap. An FBI man contacted George, saying he was a fellow spy. He said he wanted to get together with George. The two of them met in a hotel room. George didn't know it, but the meeting was being taped by FBI agents. During the meeting, George talked at length about his work as a spy.

That was all the agents needed. They arrested George and charged him with espionage. George insisted it was all a mistake. He said he had just been making up the stories about spying. He claimed he had never helped the Russians. "I have never, never had anything to do with them," he said. "And I will repeat that until I die, or until I clear my name."

The jury listened to George's story, but they didn't believe him. They found him guilty. And so the "perfect spy" became a prisoner for life.

If you have been timed while reading this article, enter your reading time below. Then turn to the Words-per-Minute Table on page 120 and look up your reading speed (words per minute). Enter your reading speed on the graph on page 121.

Reading Time: Selection 1

_____ : _____
MINUTES   SECONDS

UNDERSTANDING IDEAS Circle the letter of the best answer.

1. **Which of the following statements about George Trofimoff is FALSE?**

   A His parents were Russian.

   B George grew up in Russia.

   C His mother died when he was young.

   D He became very close to Igor Susemihl.

2. **When did George become a Russian spy?**

   F after Igor Susemihl came to him with a bold plan

   G while he bagged groceries in Florida

   H when Vasili Mitrokhin defected to the American side

   J before he rose to a position of power as an intelligence officer

3. **George was able to gather 50,000 pages of secret documents because**

   A no one else worked in his area

   B Vasili Mitrokhin kept his secrets

   C he was a highly trusted officer

   D another American was helping him

4. **What can the reader conclude about George based on when and where he was finally arrested?**

   F He still had access to important information.

   G He had moved his base of operations to Florida.

   H He was now spying for a friend at the FBI.

   J He was no longer selling secrets to Russia.

SUMMARIZE For each blank, choose the word that best completes the meaning of the paragraph.

contacted	arrested	photographed
priest	documents	intelligence

Born in Germany to Russian parents, George Trofimoff became a high-ranking _____

officer in the United States Army. George was still in

close contact with his boyhood friend Igor, a Russian

Orthodox _____. At some point,

he was _____ by Igor and asked to

become a spy for Russia. Over the course of 25 years,

George _____ about 50,000 pages

of classified _____. Eventually, he

was _____ after being trapped by

an undercover FBI agent.

IF YOU WERE THERE What would you do if you suspected that your friend was spying for another country? Write a brief paragraph explaining your actions. Be sure to include examples from the story in your response.

_____

_____

_____

_____

_____

Trouble for the FBI

Something was wrong, and FBI officials knew it. Somebody was leaking secrets to the Russians. That was the only explanation for it. Time after time, secret operations were being compromised. The FBI had already uncovered several spies—Americans who were secretly working for the Russians. But there had to be at least one more. In 2000, the FBI set out to discover who it was.

FBI workers made up a list of all the people involved in the failed FBI missions. They searched for patterns. They looked to see who had access to information in all the cases. One name they came up with was Robert Hanssen.

Hanssen was not a very likely suspect. He seemed like an honest, hard-working man who lived a quiet life with his wife Bonnie and their six children. Most spies are paid a lot of money to betray their country. So investigators checked to see if Hanssen seemed to have extra money. He didn't. He didn't drive a fancy car or take lavish vacations. He didn't gamble. He didn't drink. His house was nice but not spectacular. He was active in the Catholic Church and he enjoyed walking his dog, and that was about it. All in all, he seemed like the last person on earth who would be a double agent.

There was one irregularity in Hanssen's file. In 1994, he was caught working at another agent's computer. But Hanssen said he was just checking the security system. Hanssen was a computer expert, so his story made sense. No one thought much about it.

FBI workers concluded that another man was probably the spy. This man lived near Hanssen, but the two men were not connected in any way. The FBI started watching this other man very closely.

Then, in November 2000, the FBI got new information. A Russian informant told them that the spy they were seeking called himself "B." The informant even had a tape with B's voice on it. When officers heard the tape, they couldn't believe it. The voice sounded just like Hanssen's.

That alone was not enough proof. But soon the informant produced a bag that B had used to carry some secret documents. The fingerprints on the bag belonged to Robert Hanssen.

Now the FBI knew that Hanssen was the spy. They wanted to catch him in the act, so they began to watch his every move. They saw him leave a piece of tape on a signpost as a signal to his Russian contacts that he had some documents to deliver. At another site, they found $50,000 that the Russians were leaving as a payment for him. On February 18, 2001, they saw Hanssen approach a bridge in a Virginia park. He was carrying a plastic bag filled with top-secret documents. They waited while he hid the bag under the bridge. Then they drew their guns, surrounded him, and placed him under arrest.

It turned out that Hanssen had been working for the Russians for 15 years. During that time, he had been given access to many of America's most closely guarded secrets. He had sold virtually all of them to the Russians. He had also passed along the names of Russian agents who were spying for America. At least two of these double agents had been killed after Hanssen revealed their identities.

Friends and neighbors were shocked to learn the truth about Robert Hanssen. Even Hanssen's wife hadn't known what he was doing. Everyone began searching for clues that would explain why this mild-mannered family man had betrayed his country.

Hanssen had been paid a substantial amount of money by the Russians. They had given him $600,000 in cash, plus three diamonds. But Hanssen hadn't spent much of this money. Apparently, money was not his primary motive.

David Vise, author of the book *The Bureau and the Mole: The Unmasking of Robert Philip Hanssen, the Most Dangerous Double Agent in FBI History*, suggested that Hanssen had always resented his fellow FBI workers. Indeed, they had sometimes made fun of him because he was so humorless. In fact, some called him "Dr. Death."

"He felt like an outsider," said Vise. "He felt angry and he felt that his brilliance was being overlooked. And he felt much smarter than the people around him." So perhaps Hanssen's spying was a bitter attempt to show his superiority or to hurt those who had shown disrespect for him.

In any case, Hanssen's activities were a disaster for the FBI. They charged him with 15 counts of espionage and conspiracy. They talked about seeking the death penalty for him. Hanssen decided to avoid that by pleading guilty. The court spared his life but sentenced him to life in prison.

Now that Robert Hanssen has been apprehended, he is no longer a threat to America. But there may be others like him still at large. As retired FBI worker David Major says, "Spying is alive and well. As we speak, someone somewhere is passing information."

If you have been timed while reading this article, enter your reading time below. Then turn to the Words-per-Minute Table on page 120 and look up your reading speed (words per minute). Enter your reading speed on the graph on page 121.

Reading Time: Selection 2

_____ : _____
MINUTES   SECONDS

UNDERSTANDING IDEAS Circle the letter of the best answer.

1. **Robert Hanssen seemed an unlikely suspect because**

   A he seemed honest and hardworking

   B he did not live an extravagant lifestyle

   C he was a family man with a wife and six children

   D all of the above

2. **What was the only irregularity about Hanssen's file as an FBI agent?**

   F He was active in the Catholic Church.

   G Hanssen kept to himself and had few friends.

   H He had been caught using another agent's computer.

   J He had been checking the security system of another computer.

3. **What was the confirmation that Hanssen was, in fact, spying for Russia?**

   A A Russian informant gave the FBI Hanssen's name and address.

   B Hanssen's fingerprints were on a bag used by agent "B."

   C Hanssen was seen walking his dog.

   D Hanssen had a wife and six children.

4. **David Vise concluded that Hanssen became a spy because**

   F he needed to make a lot of money

   G he felt unappreciated by his peers

   H he wanted a nicer home

   J all of the above

SUMMARIZE For each blank, choose the word that best completes the meaning of the paragraph.

leaking	arrest	
		pleaded
documents	information	

FBI officials knew that someone on the inside was

_____ information to the

Russians. Suspecting Robert Hanssen, the FBI observed

him leaving signals for Russian counterparts when

he had _____ to sell.

Agents saw Hanssen leave a bag full of secret

_____ under a bridge in

Virginia. Officials were then able to make

an _____. Hanssen

_____ guilty to the charges and

will spend the rest of his life behind bars.

IF YOU WERE THERE Pretend that you are an FBI agent investigating a spy like Robert Hanssen. Write a brief paragraph describing your actions. Be sure to include examples from the story in your response.

_____

_____

_____

_____

_____

_____

USE CONTEXT CLUES When you read, you may find a word whose meaning is unfamiliar to you. When that happens, you can look up the word's meaning in the dictionary. You can also find out what the word means by looking for context clues. These are words or sentences that come before or after the word. Context clues can be words with the same or opposite meanings as the unfamiliar word. They may also be an example or definition of the unfamiliar word.

Read each excerpt from the stories you just read. Circle the letter with the best meaning of the underlined word.

1. **He was put in charge of a special office in Germany. It was a place where Russian defectors were interviewed. The defectors knew a lot of secrets about Russia's government.**

   A spies

   B soldiers

   C people who change sides

   D people who are running from the police

2. **Also, he was the top man in the office. So none of his colleagues asked questions if they saw him looking through secret papers.**

   F coworkers

   G security guards

   H secret Russian contacts

   J American double agents

3. **They arrested George and charged him with espionage. George insisted it was all a mistake. He said he had just been making up the stories about spying.**

   A cheating

   B stealing

   C lying

   D spying

4. **Something was wrong, and FBI officials knew it. Somebody was leaking secrets to the Russians. That was the only explanation for it. Time after time, secret operations were being compromised.**

   F endangered

   G lost

   H cooperative

   J successful

5. **Now that Robert Hanssen has been apprehended, he is no longer a threat to America. But there may be others like him still at large.**

   A executed

   B captured

   C missing

   D worried

PUT WORDS INTO CONTEXT Complete the paragraph using the underlined words from the exercise on this page.

The business of _____ is a

very serious one in the United States. Our national

security can be _____ as a result.

In George Trofimoff's case, he ran an office in Germany

that interviewed Russian _____ .

Trofimoff gained a lot of information about

Russian secrets in that job. None of Trofimoff's

_____ suspected him because he

was in a highly respected position.

PREFIXES A prefix is one or more letters added to the beginning of a word to change its meaning. For example, the prefix *re-* means "again." The word *assign* means "to appoint to a post or duty." So, when you add the prefix *re-* to the beginning of the word *assign*, you get *reassign*, which means "to appoint to a post again."

Use a dictionary to find the meaning of each prefix below. Match the prefix with its meaning on the right. Examples for each definition are included in italics. Write the letter of the correct definition on the line. **One of the definitions will be used twice.**

_____	**1.** mis-	**A**	do the opposite of: *disapprove*
_____	**2.** un-	**B**	the part in the middle: *midstream*
_____	**3.** re-	**C**	badly, wrongly: *misunderstand*
_____	**4.** dis-	**D**	again: *revisit*
_____	**5.** mid-	**E**	against: *antiwar*
_____	**6.** in-	**F**	not: *indecisive, uncooperative*
_____	**7.** pre-	**G**	before: *preview*
_____	**8.** anti-		

WRITE DEFINITIONS In the exerceise below, underline the prefix and write the new meaning of the word on the line provided.

1. in + flexible = inflexible

definition: _____

2. un + suspecting = unsuspecting

definition: _____

3. dis + respect = disrespect

definition: _____

4. mid + town = midtown

definition: _____

5. pre + judge = prejudge

definition: _____

6. mis + information = misinformation

definition: _____

7. anti + depressant = antidepressant

definition: _____

8. re + visit = revisit

definition: _____

FIND THE PURPOSE You already know that authors write to inform or teach, to persuade or convince, or to entertain. You also know that many times authors write for more than one purpose. Advertisements, for example, can fit all three purposes for writing. The ad may inform you about a product or service you can buy. It attempts to persuade you to buy it, and often, ads are entertaining so that they appeal readily to a large number of people.

Review the chart below. Then answer the questions.

Author's Purpose		
to inform (teach)	**to persuade (convince)**	**to entertain (amuse)**
• textbook	• editorials	• fictional stories
• newspaper and magazine articles	• advertisements	• poems
• nonfiction stories/books	• position papers (for or against an issue)	• humorous essays, books, or cartoons
• reviews (movies, books, music, and so on)	• lawyer's briefs (arguments)	• anecdotes (personal stories)

1. **"The Perfect Spy" is an example of a story that should appear under which heading?**
   - **A** to inform
   - **B** to persuade
   - **C** to entertain
   - **D** all of the above

2. **What is the primary purpose behind David Vise's nonfiction book, *The Bureau and the Mole: The Unmasking of Robert Philip Hanssen, the Most Dangerous Double Agent in FBI History*?**
   - **F** to inform
   - **G** to persuade
   - **H** to entertain
   - **J** all of the above

3. **If a concerned citizen wrote a newspaper editorial about security breaches in the FBI, what would the primary purpose be?**
   - **A** to inform
   - **B** to persuade
   - **C** to entertain
   - **D** all of the above

4. **If someone wrote a novel called *Life in the FBI*, what would its purpose be?**
   - **F** to inform
   - **G** to persuade
   - **H** to entertain
   - **J** all of the above

WRITE WITH A PURPOSE Write a topic sentence about the different aspects of spies and/or spying for each of the purposes you reviewed in this lesson.

to inform: _____

_____

to persuade: _____

_____

to entertain: _____

_____

DRAW CONCLUSIONS You draw conclusions every day based on the information available to you. If you see police cars in front of your house, you may conclude that somebody reported a crime or an emergency. You may rush home just in case a member of your family needs your help. Or, you may decide to wait until the police leave. In big and little ways, you act on your own conclusions all the time.

Read the following paragraph about spies and then choose the best answer to each question.

[1] Espionage between Russia and the United States became very intense during the Cold War. [2] The Cold War was a period when the two superpowers waged a war of ideas and world views. [3] Each side believed that its economic and political system should be the model for all nations of the world. [4] In addition, both countries were concerned for their own security. [5] As a result, each side used spies to find out what the other was planning to do.

1. **Which conclusion can you draw based on the paragraph above?**

   A Before the Cold War, Russia and the United States were on friendly terms.

   B The United States and Russia had similar ideas about government.

   C The Cold War was between two opposing political and economic systems.

   D Spying is a rare practice among democratic and communist governments.

2. **Which conclusion would United States agents make if a Russian spy were caught passing blueprints of a United States weapon?**

   F If the Russians got the blueprints, they would build a similar weapon.

   G The Russian spy was working for the United States.

   H The United States was successful in fooling the Russians.

   J The United States is not paying its spies enough money.

JUDGE THE EVIDENCE When you draw conclusions, you have to weigh the evidence. Choose the best answer.

1. **Which statement supports the conclusion that both the United States and Russia used spies?**

   A The defectors knew a lot of secrets about Russia's government.

   B Hanssen passed along names of Russian agents who were spying for America.

   C George Trofimoff gave top-secret documents to the Russians.

   D The FBI wanted to catch Hanssen in the act.

2. **Which statement supports the conclusion that money is not always the primary motive for spying?**

   F Investigators checked to see if Hanssen had extra money.

   G George Trofimoff was arrested in Florida.

   H George Trofimoff rose to a position of power.

   J Hanssen received $600,000 from the Russians, but he didn't spend much of the money.

YOUR OWN CONCLUSION Do you think spying for the enemy would be a satisfying career? State your conclusions and support them with examples from both stories.

_____

_____

_____

_____

_____

_____

In the Wind

Kathleen Soliah knew she was in trouble. The FBI was closing in on her. On September 18, 1975, FBI agents arrested two of her friends. Kathleen realized she was next on the list. So she packed up a few of her belongings and left the San Francisco house where she had been staying. She slipped out into the streets, leaving behind no clue as to where she was headed. For the next 23 years, the authorities didn't know where she had gone. She was, as they put it, "in the wind."

With Kathleen in hiding, the case against her could not be closed. She stood accused of a very serious crime. According to authorities, she had planted two large pipe bombs under police cars. Luckily, officers had discovered them before they exploded. But the bombs had clearly been designed to kill people. They were packed full of nails and loaded with explosives. One was particularly lethal. Said one official, "It was one of the biggest pipe bombs, if not the biggest, in the history of the United States."

The police connected Kathleen to the bombs by tracing the parts used to make them. A salesman remembered selling Kathleen the parts. Authorities weren't surprised that she was involved in terrorist activities. They knew she was involved with members of the

Symbionese Liberation Army, or SLA. This group believed the U.S. government was so corrupt that nothing could fix it. They called for the violent overthrow of the government.

Kathleen hadn't started out as a radical. She grew up in a conservative family. In high school she had seemed like the model child. She belonged to Future Teachers of America. She won a Service and Spirit award. In 1968, she even supported Republican Richard Nixon for president. But all that changed in the early 1970s. Kathleen was attracted to the SLA. She became more and more extreme in her thinking. The authorities had a tape of a speech she had made in June of 1975. In it, she called the police "pigs" and told the SLA, "I am with you!"

In planting the bombs, she had gone too far. But she couldn't be prosecuted until she could be found. And no one seemed to know where she was. The police and the FBI kept looking, but after a while they ran out of leads. They had no idea what alias she was using. They didn't know if she had cut her long red hair—or perhaps dyed it a different color. They didn't know if she was pursuing any of her old hobbies, such as acting, or had taken up brand new ones. She could have been in any state, in any city, in any small town. She could have fled the country altogether. There was just no way for them to know.

It turned out that Kathleen hadn't fled the country. She had made her way to Minneapolis, Minnesota, where she used the name Sara Jane Olson. This name was a smart choice. Minneapolis was full of Olsons. The local phone book had 14 pages worth of people with that last name. Sara Jane was one Olson among thousands.

Telling everyone she was from California, she got a job as a cook and began to get involved in local theatre productions. She never did cut her long red hair, nor did she completely give up her interest in politics. But she soon fell in love with a Harvard-educated doctor named Fred Peterson. They got married, and "Sara Jane" settled into a very comfortable life.

In the past, Kathleen had scorned the way upper-middle-class people lived. But now she lived happily in a $300,000 home. She gave dinner parties and participated in community theatre. She raised three daughters, driving them to school events and soccer games in her gold minivan. She read to the blind and attended church. In this tidy new life, she never told anyone her real identity. Even her husband had no idea who she really was.

But Sara Jane's past caught up with her in the spring of 1999. In May of that year, the TV program *America's Most Wanted* profiled Kathleen Soliah. It showed photos of Kathleen from 1975 and offered viewers a sketch of what she might currently look like. The show generated 20 tips. Nineteen proved to be dead ends, but one led authorities

directly to the fancy house of "Sara Jane Olson" in Minneapolis, Minnesota. Kathleen was in her car when authorities pulled her over. "Hey, Kathy, how's it going?" one officer said to her. "You want to go by Kathy or Sara Jane?"

"I want to speak to my lawyer," was her reply.

Fred Peterson was stunned to learn that his wife was Kathleen Soliah. "He couldn't believe it," reported one observer. The three Olson daughters were equally shocked, as were friends of the family. "The Sara Jane I know is nothing like this Kathleen Soliah fugitive," said Andy Dawkins.

But in fact, Kathleen Soliah and Sara Jane Olson were the same person. In the fall of 2001, this terrorist-turned-homemaker finally had her day in court. She pleaded guilty to planting the pipe bombs all those years ago.

"I'm still the same person I was then," she said. "I believe in democracy for all people, and all the things that that entails. And I don't have any regrets. I'm proud."

The judge sentenced her to 20 years in prison.

If you have been timed while reading this article, enter your reading time below. Then turn to the Words-per-Minute Table on page 120 and look up your reading speed (words per minute). Enter your reading speed on the graph on page 121.

Reading Time: Selection 1

_____ : _____
   MINUTES   SECONDS

UNDERSTANDING IDEAS Circle the letter of the best answer.

1. **What does the phrase "in the wind" mean?**

   A The FBI is hot on the trail of a criminal.

   B Bad weather has prevented an FBI arrest.

   C Someone has disappeared without a trace.

   D There are rumors about where criminals are hiding.

2. **Which statement compares Soliah's early life with her later life?**

   F Soliah was accused of planting pipe bombs, but no one thought she did it.

   G Soliah lived with a comfortable amount of money in a very nice neighborhood.

   H Soliah had a husband and three children who did not know her true identity.

   J Soliah joined a violent terrorist group but later led a conservative life in Minnesota.

3. **Why had the FBI been unable to prosecute Kathleen Soliah?**

   A They could not find her.

   B She had three daughters.

   C She moved to Minneapolis, Minnesota.

   D They did not have enough evidence against her.

4. **What can the reader conclude from the following statement by Kathleen Soliah?**

   > "I believe in democracy for all people, and all the things that that entails. And I don't have any regrets. I'm proud"

   F Soliah hopes the U.S. government undergoes reform.

   G Soliah is glad that she was involved with the SLA many years ago.

   H Soliah would not plant pipe bombs ever again.

   J Soliah is sorry she was caught.

SUMMARIZE For each blank, choose the word that best completes the meaning of the paragraph.

terrorist	profile	name
disappeared	caught	husband

Kathleen Soliah had become associated with the SLA, a _____ organization. Soliah knew she was close to getting _____ by the FBI. So she left her home and _____. She moved to Minnesota and changed her _____, got a job, fell in love, and got married. Her new _____ knew nothing of her past life. Years later, the TV show "America's Most Wanted" did a _____ on Soliah, and she was finally caught and put in prison.

IF YOU WERE THERE How would you react if you found out devastating information about your mother's past? Write a brief paragraph explaining your thoughts and actions. Be sure to include examples from the story to support your response.

_____

_____

_____

_____

_____

Running from Her Past

Theresa Grosso had a secret. Her friends all thought she was a gentle, peace-loving woman who grew organic vegetables, drank carrot juice, and spent countless hours home-schooling her son. While this was true, there was another side to Theresa that few people knew about. As a young woman, Theresa had lived a wild, undisciplined life. She had taken drugs and abused alcohol. And on the night of September 27, 1969, under the influence of several substances, she had pulled out a gun and shot a man.

It was a murder that made no sense. The man hadn't done anything to Theresa. She didn't even know his name. When the drugs and alcohol wore off, she couldn't remember the shooting—or anything else that had happened that night. Still, she had killed a man and so the police arrested her on a charge of first-degree murder. A jury found her guilty, and the judge sentenced her to life in prison.

Theresa didn't want to spend the rest of her life behind bars, so she immediately began planning her escape. Over the next six years, she escaped from prison three times. Each time she was caught and returned to the Maryland Correctional Institution for Women. On August 30, 1979, she escaped a fourth time. This time the police didn't catch her. But Theresa knew that the only way to stay out of prison was to be careful, keep a low profile, and always be ready to run.

As a fugitive, Theresa couldn't share her story with many people. She did tell the truth to one man, however. He was Bill Palm, and he fell in love with Theresa while she was on the run. Bill didn't care about Theresa's past. He was willing to go anywhere and do anything so long as he could be with her. He and Theresa moved to Florida, where Theresa called herself Patricia Leno. In 1980, they had a son, whom they named Richard.

Theresa wanted desperately to be a good mother. She became a vegetarian and began reading books about religion and spirituality. One thing she couldn't do, however, was give Richard roots in a community. She was afraid the police would catch her if she stayed in one place too long. So over the next few years, she and Bill moved with Richard to Georgia, Tennessee, Colorado, Oregon, and finally New Mexico.

In New Mexico, they settled into a commune called City of the Sun. Theresa worked in the greenhouse while Bill cut and split firewood. It was a calm, quiet existence, and Theresa loved it. "I was living the life I'd always wanted to live," she said.

Still, she couldn't completely forget her past. For one thing, she felt great remorse for the murder she had committed. As she later said, "I took a life. That's still the hardest thing. I wish it had never happened. All the other things I've done in life, you can kind of say you learn from them, but this . . . . I pray about that all the time. It's a hard situation to live with."

The other source of distress in Theresa's life was her fear of getting caught. She didn't want to be separated from Bill and Richard, and she didn't want to go back to prison. So she was constantly looking over her shoulder, watching for signs that the police were headed her way.

In 1983, Theresa, Bill, and Richard moved again, this time to Arizona. Taking the names Sheila and David Guest, they became caretakers on a ranch. Theresa made friends with everyone there, and when a neighbor named Carole Cox fell ill, Theresa nursed her back to health. "I believe she saved my life," said Cox.

In 1987, Theresa and her family moved on to Hawaii, where Theresa changed her first name to Rose.

By this time, Richard was old enough to be in school, but Theresa chose to home-school him. She didn't want him out of her sight—and she didn't want to leave a paper trail when they moved again. Richard had no idea that his mother was a murderer and a fugitive. To him, she was just Mom.

Eventually, however, Richard learned the truth. A friend saw a TV show about fugitives at large. Theresa was one of the people highlighted, and the friend recognized her. Theresa realized that her idyllic life with Bill and Richard was over. If she continued to live with them, they would have to go deeper into hiding and then Richard wouldn't have any sort of normal life. So Theresa gathered all her courage and said goodbye to them both.

Theresa went back to Florida, where she made friends with a man named Jay Herron. Believing she could trust him, Theresa shared with him the secrets of her past. Herron called the FBI, and on December 1, 1998, officers arrested Theresa and sent her back to prison.

This time, there was no way Theresa Grosso could escape. She was kept in an isolated cell surrounded by high walls and razor wire. She was allowed out for exercise, but only when wearing leg irons.

Although Theresa still felt terrible about having taken a man's life, she did not regret her years as a fugitive. If she hadn't escaped, she said, "I wouldn't have had Richard. I wouldn't have had the life I had for 19 years. If I had stayed here for those 19 years, I would never have touched base with the good inside of me."

If you have been timed while reading this article, enter your reading time below. Then turn to the Words-per-Minute Table on page 120 and look up your reading speed (words per minute). Enter your reading speed on the graph on page 121.

Reading Time: Selection 2

_____ : _____
MINUTES   SECONDS

UNDERSTANDING IDEAS Circle the letter of the best answer.

1. **Which statement best describes Theresa Grosso's life before she committed murder?**

   A She was out of control.

   B She studied a lot in school.

   C She was afraid of being caught by police.

   D She lived a quiet life and enjoyed gardening.

2. **What could Theresa NOT do for her son because she was on the run?**

   F stay at home with him

   G homeschool him

   H allow Richard to help in the garden

   J allow Richard to settle into a neighborhood

3. **What statement belongs in the empty box?**

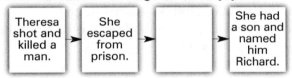

   A She called herself Sheila Guest.

   B She moved to New Mexico.

   C She met Bill Palm and fell in love.

   D She lived in the City of the Sun.

4. **What can the reader conclude about why Theresa left Bill and Richard?**

   F Theresa wanted Richard to have a normal life.

   G Theresa decided to go back to her old ways.

   H She was tired of family life.

   J They slowed her down.

SUMMARIZE For each blank, choose the word that best completes the meaning of the paragraph.

moved	influence	truth
recognized	prison	escape

Under the _____ of drugs and alcohol, Theresa Grosso had shot and killed a man. Theresa managed to _____ from prison after trying four times. She met Bill Palm and told him the _____ about her past. The pair, along with their son, _____ from place to place for years. Finally, one of her son's friends _____ her on a TV program. She left Bill and Richard and moved back to Florida. There she was arrested and sent back to _____.

IF YOU WERE THERE Write a brief paragraph explaining what your life would be like if you were running from the law. Be sure to include examples from the story to support your response.

_____

_____

_____

_____

_____

_____

USE CONTEXT CLUES When you read, you may find a word whose meaning is unfamiliar to you. When that happens, you can look up the word's meaning in the dictionary. You can also find out what the word means by looking for context clues. These are words or sentences that come before or after the word. Context clues can be words with the same or opposite meanings as the unfamiliar word. They may also be an example or definition of the unfamiliar word.

Read each excerpt from the stories you just read. Circle the letter with the best meaning of the underlined word.

1. **This group [the SLA] believed the U.S. government was so <u>corrupt</u> that nothing could fix it. They called for the violent overthrow of the government.**
   A big
   B evil
   C right wing
   D well organized

2. **Kathleen hadn't started out as a <u>radical</u>. She grew up in a conservative family. In high school, she had seemed like the model child.**
   F campaigner
   G criminal
   H extremist
   J reformer

3. **They [the FBI] had no idea what <u>alias</u> she was using. . . . She had made her way to Minneapolis, Minnesota, where she used the name Sara Jane Olson.**
   A drugs
   B fake name
   C stolen car
   D terrorist connections

4. **But Theresa knew the only way to stay out of prison was to be careful, keep a low profile, and always be ready to run. As a <u>fugitive</u>, Theresa couldn't share her story with many people.**
   F alcoholic
   G escapee
   H murderer
   J prisoner

5. **Still, she couldn't completely forget her past. For one thing, she felt great <u>remorse</u> for the murder she had committed. As she later said, "I took a life. That's still the hardest thing."**
   A regret
   B anger
   C surprise
   D fear

PUT WORDS INTO CONTEXT Complete the paragraph using the underlined words from the exercise on this page.

Kathleen Soliah was a _____ from the law. So was Theresa Grosso. The difference is that Grosso felt tremendous _____ for her past, and Soliah didn't. Soliah was a _____ who tried to make her statement by putting pipe bombs under police cars. Grosso was different, but her crime was senseless as well. Both women used an _____ and started new lives for themselves. In the end, both were captured by police.

ROOTS IN NUMBER WORDS As you have learned, one way of finding out the meaning of a word is by looking for its root. If you know the meaning of a root word, you can often decipher the meaning of a word you don't know. Many of the number words we use in English have Latin and Greek roots. The chart below shows some examples.

number	Greek	Latin	examples
one or single	mono	uni	unified, monopolize
two or pair	di	bi, duo	bicycle, duo
three	tri	tri	triad, triangle
ten	dec, deca, deka	deci	decade, decimal
thousands	khilo (kilo)	milli	million, kilometer

Read the complete paragraphs. For each numbered blank, refer to the word choices in the right column. Choose a word that best completes the meaning of the paragraph.

Cases of escaped convicts have kept the police hunting

for (1) _____. More than two

(2) _____ ago, a woman named

Kathleen Soliah realized that in order to avoid being

arrested by the FBI, she had to disappear. Soliah was

accused of placing a (3) _____

of pipe bombs under police cars. The SLA is

(4) _____ in its view that

American government is corrupt.

Theresa Grosso was also a fugitive from the law. Her

crime was first-degree murder. Grosso had managed to

escape from prison (5) _____

times. All seemed well until a TV program profiled Grosso.

Then she became one of (6) _____

of fugitives who have been captured.

1. **A** centuries
   B decimeters
   C kilometers
   D millions

2. **F** monopolize
   G kilometer
   H decimals
   J decades

3. **A** decimal
   B pair
   C bicycle
   D quad

4. **F** cent
   G decimal
   H hectogram
   J unified

5. **A** one
   B two
   C four
   D kilo

6. **F** pair
   G single
   H kilometer
   J hundreds

ORGANIZE THE FACTS To understand a passage, you should ask questions about the text before, during, and after reading and then look for answers. While you are reading, know how and where to look for answers to questions. Sometimes the answer might be stated directly in the passage; other times you need to put ideas or information together to come up with the answer. Then sometimes the answer may not be in the passage at all, but may be something you already know.

Look at the chart below. Then answer the questions on the right.

Question-Answer Relationships	
Question	**How to Answer**
• Where was Kathleen Soliah living when two of her friends were arrested?	Question words such as who, where, and when usually indicate that the answer is right there in the passage.
• What was the reason that Soliah planted the pipe bombs?	The question words what and why sometimes require you to think and to search the passage.
• Why do fugitives change their names and move from place to place?	A general question like this is about something you probably know. You can come up with the answer on your own.
• How do you think people would react if Kathleen Soliah were to write a book called What's Wrong with America?	A question that asks what you think requires you to use what you already know and what the author tells you. You will make an inference or draw a conclusion.

1. **Which question can you answer by looking for a direct statement from the story?**

   A What name did Soliah use in Minnesota?

   B Why was Soliah so critical of the United States?

   C Why do some people use violence to make a statement?

   D Did Soliah think she would ever get caught? Why or why not?

2. **Which question can you answer by thinking and searching?**

   F What did the SLA want to accomplish?

   G Do you think Soliah should have been sent to prison?

   H How do you think Soliah's children reacted when they learned her real identity?

   J How do you think Soliah's new life compares with her past?

3. **Which question requires you to use what you already know and what the author tells you?**

   A How long was Soliah on the run?

   B Why do you think Soliah said she was "proud" of her past?

   C What kind of family did Soliah have when she was growing up?

   D When did Fred Peterson find out that the FBI was hunting for his wife?

WRITE YOUR OWN QUESTIONS Write two questions about each of the stories in this unit. For each question, explain how you would find the answer.

_____

_____

_____

_____

MAKE PREDICTIONS You can make predictions, or educated guesses, based on what you already know. For example, you already know that people who have committed crimes often try to hide from police like Theresa Grosso did. Based on this knowledge, you can reasonably predict that there are many more fugitives from justice on the loose.

Read this passage and answer the following questions based on what you know after reading the stories.

Wanted

[1] Raymond Abbott Baerga is one of the U.S. Marshals' Top 15 Most Wanted Fugitives. [2] He escaped from a maximum security detention facility several years ago on July 3, 1992. [3] Baerga was awaiting sentencing after pleading guilty to weapons smuggling. [4] The name that Baerga sometimes goes by is Robo-Cop. [5] He is a white male, weighs approximately 160 pounds, and is 5'10" tall. [6] He has black hair and brown eyes. [7] Baerga is 41 years old. [8] He should be considered armed and dangerous.

1. **Which of the following do you predict the U.S. Marshals Service recommends if you encounter Raymond Abbot Baerga?**

   A Try to convince him to turn himself in.

   B Don't do anything—he's dangerous.

   C Report any information to a U.S. Marshals Service District Office.

   D Stay inside and keep low to the ground.

2. **What do you predict that Baerga will do if he knows he is on the Most Wanted list?**

   F kill himself

   G take a hostage

   H turn himself in

   J go deeper into hiding

JUDGE THE BASIS OF A PREDICTION For predictions to be reasonably accurate, they must be based on what you know as factual information. Choose the best answer.

1. **Which sentence from the passage at the left helps you predict that Baerga is good at hiding out?**

   A Sentence 1

   B Sentence 2

   C Sentence 3

   D Sentence 4

2. **Which sentence from the passage helps you predict that the U.S. Marshals office considers catching Baerga a top priority?**

   F Sentence 1

   G Sentence 2

   H Sentence 3

   J Sentence 4

PREDICT WHAT YOU WOULD DO Write a brief paragraph explaining what you would do if a coworker told you she might be dating someone who is wanted by police. Use examples from the stories you just read to explain your own predictions.

_____

_____

_____

_____

_____

_____

Words-per-Minute Table

If you were timed while reading, find your reading time in the column on the left. Find the unit and number of the story across the top of the chart. Follow the time row across to its intersection with the column of the story. This is your reading speed. Go to the next page to plot your progress.

Unit → Selection → Time	1-1	1-2	2-1	2-2	3-1	3-2	4-1	4-2	5-1	5-2	6-1	6-2	7-1	7-2	8-1	8-2	9-1	9-2	10-1	10-2
(Word count)	882	873	806	961	806	842	846	839	775	824	874	867	709	789	796	885	810	833	906	921
1:20	662	655	605	721	605	632	635	629	581	618	656	650	532	592	597	664	608	625	680	691
1:40	529	524	484	577	484	505	508	503	465	494	524	520	425	473	478	531	486	500	544	553
2:00	441	437	403	481	403	421	423	420	388	412	437	434	355	395	398	443	405	417	453	461
2:20	378	374	345	412	345	361	363	360	332	353	375	372	304	338	341	379	347	357	388	395
2:40	331	327	302	360	302	316	317	315	291	309	328	325	266	296	299	332	304	312	340	345
3:00	294	291	269	320	269	281	282	280	258	275	291	289	236	263	265	295	270	278	302	307
3:20	265	262	242	288	242	253	254	252	233	247	262	260	213	237	239	266	243	250	272	276
3:40	241	238	220	262	220	230	231	229	211	225	238	236	193	215	217	241	221	227	247	251
4:00	221	218	202	240	202	211	212	210	194	206	219	217	177	197	199	221	203	208	227	230
4:20	204	201	186	222	186	194	195	194	179	190	202	200	164	182	184	204	187	192	209	213
4:40	189	187	173	206	173	180	181	180	166	177	187	186	152	169	171	190	174	179	194	197
5:00	176	175	161	192	161	168	169	168	155	165	175	173	142	158	159	177	162	167	181	184
5:20	165	164	151	180	151	158	159	157	145	155	164	163	133	148	149	166	152	156	170	173
5:40	156	154	142	170	142	149	149	148	137	145	154	153	125	139	140	156	143	147	160	163
6:00	147	146	134	160	134	140	141	140	129	137	146	145	118	132	133	148	135	139	151	154
6:20	139	138	127	152	127	133	134	132	122	130	138	137	112	125	126	140	128	132	143	145
6:40	132	131	121	144	121	126	127	126	116	124	131	130	106	118	119	133	122	125	136	138
7:00	126	125	115	137	115	120	121	120	111	118	125	124	101	113	114	126	116	119	129	132
7:20	120	119	110	131	110	115	115	114	106	112	119	118	97	108	109	121	110	114	124	126
7:40	115	114	105	125	105	110	110	109	101	107	114	113	92	103	104	115	106	109	118	120
8:00	110	109	101	120	101	105	106	105	97	103	109	108	89	99	100	111	101	104	113	115
8:20	106	105	97	115	97	101	102	101	93	99	105	104	85	95	96	106	97	100	109	111
8:40	102	101	93	111	93	97	98	97	89	95	101	100	82	91	92	102	93	96	105	106
9:00	98	97	90	107	90	94	94	93	86	92	97	96	79	88	88	98	90	93	101	102
9:20	95	94	86	103	86	90	91	90	83	88	94	93	76	85	85	95	87	89	97	99
9:40	91	90	83	99	83	87	88	87	80	85	90	90	73	82	82	92	84	86	94	95
10:00	88	87	81	96	81	84	85	84	78	82	87	87	71	79	80	89	81	83	91	92
10:20	85	84	78	93	78	81	82	81	75	80	85	84	69	76	77	86	78	81	88	89
10:40	83	82	76	90	76	79	79	79	73	77	82	81	66	74	75	83	76	78	85	86
11:00	80	79	73	87	73	77	77	76	70	75	79	79	64	72	72	80	74	76	82	84
11:20	78	77	71	85	71	74	75	74	68	73	77	77	63	70	70	78	71	74	80	81
11:40	76	75	69	82	69	72	73	72	66	71	75	74	61	68	68	76	69	71	78	79
12:00	74	73	67	80	67	70	71	70	65	69	73	72	59	66	66	74	68	69	76	77
12:20	72	71	65	78	65	68	69	68	63	67	71	70	57	64	65	72	66	68	73	75
12:40	70	69	64	76	64	66	67	66	61	65	69	68	56	62	63	70	64	66	72	73
13:00	68	67	62	74	62	65	65	65	60	63	67	67	55	61	61	68	62	64	70	71
13:20	66	65	60	72	60	63	63	63	58	62	66	65	53	59	60	66	61	62	68	69
13:40	65	64	59	70	59	62	62	61	57	60	64	63	52	58	58	65	59	61	66	67
14:00	63	62	58	69	58	60	60	60	55	59	62	62	51	56	57	63	58	60	65	66
14:20	62	61	56	67	56	59	59	59	54	57	61	60	49	55	56	62	57	58	63	64
14:40	60	60	55	66	55	57	58	57	53	56	60	59	48	54	54	60	55	57	62	63
15:00	59	58	54	64	54	56	56	56	52	55	58	58	47	53	53	59	54	56	60	61

Plotting Your Progress: Reading Speed

Enter your words-per-minute rate in the box above the appropriate lesson. Then place a small X on the line directly above the number of the lesson, across from the number of words per minute you read. Graph your progress by drawing a line to connect the X's.

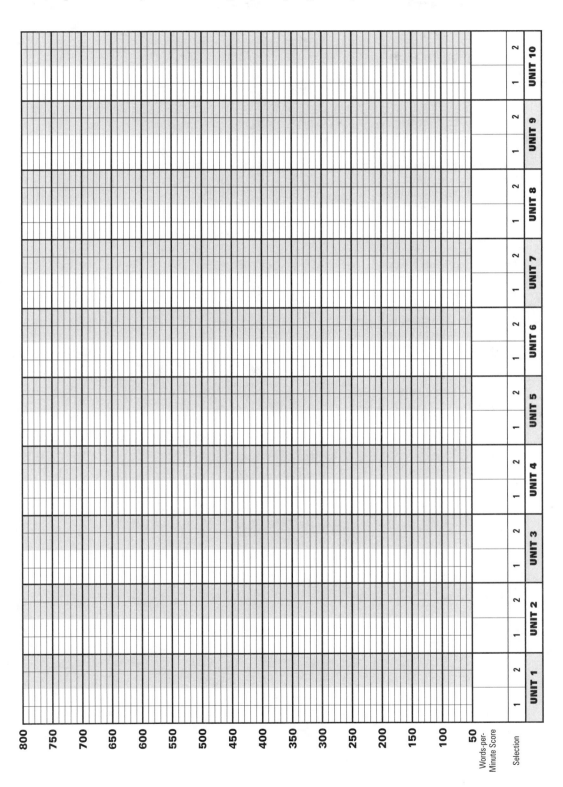

Photo Credits